Alchemy of the Oven: Earth, Air, Fire, Water, Spirit

Emilee Avink

Published by Emilee Avink, 2024.

ALCHEMY OF THE OVEN: EARTH, AIR, FIRE, WATER, SPIRIT

First edition. May 26, 2024.

Copyright © 2024 Emilee Avink.

ISBN: 979-8224247172

Written by Emilee Avink.

Also by Emilee Avink

Embracing the Witch's Shadow: A Guide to Transformation and Self-Discovery: Unlocking the Secrets of Witchcraft,
Healing and Personal Empowerment
Where Two Worlds Collide
The Infinite Loop: A Time Traveler's Search for Love
Whispers of the Guardian: Haleema's Legacy
The Pot of Plenty: Stretching Your Dollar with 50 Delicious Rice and Bean Dishes
Description for Nine Lives of Magic: Working with Your Feline Familiar
Once Upon a Feast: Fairytale Treats for Little Chefs
The Glitching Grimoire: A Tech Witch's Guide to Digital Spellcraft
The Healing Table: Crystal-Infused Meals
Buzzing with Magic: Quick & Effective Witchcraft for Busy Bees
The Witch's Daily Cup: Rituals and Recipes for Coffee Magic
Alchemy of the Oven: Earth, Air, Fire, Water, Spirit

Table of Contents

Alchemy of the Oven: Earth, Air, Fire, Water, Spirit

The Philosophy of Elemental Cooking

Welcome, fellow explorers, to the captivating world of elemental cooking! Within these pages, we embark on a journey that transcends mere sustenance. We delve into the ancient wisdom of the five elements – earth, air, fire, water, and spirit – and discover how they hold the key to unlocking a deeper connection with both food and nature.

Have you ever wondered why a perfectly roasted root vegetable feels so grounding, or why a light and airy soufflé brings a sense of pure joy? The answer lies in the subtle dance between the elements and our senses. Each element possesses unique characteristics that are reflected in the ingredients we choose, the techniques we employ, and ultimately, the experience we create on the plate.

Earth, with its solidity and warmth, embodies comfort and nourishment. **Fire**, passionate and transformative, imbues food with bold flavors and dramatic presentations. **Air**, light and fleeting, speaks of delicate textures and refreshing tastes. **Water**, adaptable and life-giving, forms the foundation of countless culinary creations. And finally, **Spirit**, the essence of creativity, encourages us to push boundaries and express our personal culinary voice.

This book is your guide to mastering the alchemy of the oven. We'll explore the essence of each element, how it translates into cooking methods and flavors, and how to weave these elements together to create truly transformative dishes. As you dive deeper, you'll discover:

- The history and cultural significance of elemental cooking
- How the elements connect to your well-being based on Traditional Chinese Medicine principles
- Techniques and recipes that bring forth the essence of each element

Prepare to be surprised. We'll not only unlock the secrets of classic dishes but also embark on culinary adventures, crafting unexpected yet harmonious flavor combinations. Whether you're a seasoned cook or just setting out on your culinary journey, elemental cooking offers a path to deepen your understanding and appreciation of food.

So, preheat your oven, gather your ingredients, and get ready to experience the magic of the five elements. Let the alchemy begin!

The Five Elements: A Journey Through Time and Culture

THE FIVE-ELEMENT THEORY, with its core elements of earth, air, fire, water, and spirit, transcends a single culture or historical period. It's a captivating tapestry woven across continents, each civilization adding its own vibrant thread.

East Meets West:

- **China:** The five elements (Wu Xing) form the foundation of Traditional Chinese Medicine, influencing everything from food to medicine. Earth represents the body, water nourishes, fire transforms, air circulates energy, and spirit embodies consciousness.

- **India:** The five elements (Panchamahabhuta) are central to Ayurveda, the ancient Indian system of holistic health. Each element is linked to specific bodily functions and influences dietary practices.

- **Greece:** Empedocles, a pre-Socratic philosopher, proposed four elements (earth, air, fire, water) as the building blocks of matter. These elements were later incorporated by Aristotle into his influential theory of nature.

Beyond the East and West:

- **Mesoamerica:** The Maya civilization utilized a five-element system that included earth, air, fire, water, and maize (a vital food source). This system was integral to their understanding of the cosmos and human well-being.

- **Native American Traditions:** Many indigenous cultures in North America held reverence for the five elements, often associating them with cardinal directions, colors, and spiritual concepts.

While the specific names and associations may vary across cultures, the underlying theme remains consistent. The five elements represent the fundamental forces that shape the natural world and influence our lives. By understanding this ancient wisdom, we can approach cooking with a deeper appreciation for the interconnectedness of food, nature, and ourselves.

This is just a brief glimpse into the rich history of the five elements. As you delve deeper into this book, we'll explore how these time-tested concepts translate into the exciting realm of elemental cooking!

The Elements and Your Well-Being: A TCM Perspective

TRADITIONAL CHINESE Medicine (TCM) views the human body as a microcosm of the universe, where balance between the five elements – earth, air, fire, water, and spirit – is key to health and well-being. Let's explore how these elements translate to our internal landscape and how food choices can support balance.

- **Earth:** Representing the physical body, stability, and grounding, earth corresponds to the Spleen and Stomach in TCM. When earth is balanced, we feel strong, nourished, and centered. Conversely, an imbalance can manifest as digestive issues, fatigue, or feelings of being ungrounded. Earthy foods like root vegetables, whole grains, and legumes are seen as building blocks for a healthy body.

- **Water:** The element of water embodies fluidity, adaptability, and our vital essence (Jing). It's linked to the Kidney and Bladder in TCM. Balanced water translates to proper hydration, strong immunity, and healthy energy flow. Imbalance can lead to dehydration, fatigue, or urinary issues. Watery foods like broths, soups, and fruits support optimal hydration and kidney function.

- **Fire:** Fire represents transformation, energy, and circulation. In TCM, it corresponds to the Heart and Small Intestine. Balanced fire translates to good digestion, healthy circulation, and a vibrant spirit. Imbalance can manifest as heartburn, anxiety, or insomnia. Spicy foods, while used sparingly, can stimulate digestion, while bitter greens can support the liver (which works with the Heart in TCM).

- **Air:** Associated with lightness, circulation, and the respiratory system, air relates to the Lungs and Large Intestine in TCM. Balanced air translates to clear breathing, efficient elimination, and a positive outlook. Imbalance can manifest as respiratory issues, constipation, or sluggishness. Airy foods like leafy greens and light grains promote healthy digestion and elimination.

- **Spirit:** The essence of creativity, consciousness, and connection to the universe, spirit is not directly linked to an organ in TCM. However, it's seen as the animating force behind the other elements. A balanced spirit manifests as joy, vitality, and a sense of purpose. Imbalance can lead to a lack of motivation, difficulty connecting with others, or a feeling of being lost. Experimenting with new and exciting flavors and presentations can nourish the spirit and spark culinary creativity.

By understanding these connections, we can use food as a tool to support our well-being and create a more balanced internal environment. Remember, TCM is a holistic system, and dietary practices should be tailored to your individual needs. Consulting a qualified TCM practitioner can provide personalized guidance on how to use food to support your specific health goals.

This knowledge of the elements, along with the recipes in this book, empowers you to create meals that are not only delicious but also contribute to your overall well-being. Let's embark on this culinary journey together!

Elemental Diets: Tailoring Your Meals to Your Needs

THE FIVE ELEMENTS OFFER a powerful lens not just for understanding cooking techniques and flavors, but also for creating meals that address your current needs. This concept forms the basis of elemental diets, a practice where food choices are made based on balancing the elements within your body.

Imagine feeling sluggish and achy – an earth imbalance. An elemental diet could incorporate grounding root vegetables and nourishing stews to bring back a sense of stability. Conversely, feeling overly stressed or anxious might point to a fire imbalance. Cooling and calming ingredients like leafy greens and cucumber salads can help restore balance.

Here's a basic approach to creating elemental meals:

1. Identify Your Needs: Reflect on your current state of being. Are you feeling sluggish (earth), overstimulated (fire), or lacking energy (water)? Consider any physical symptoms or emotional imbalances you might be experiencing.

2. Choose Elements to Support: Based on your needs, identify the element(s) you want to support. Craving grounding? Focus on earth. Feeling fiery? Look to cooling water ingredients.

3. Explore Elemental Foods: Refer to the characteristics of each element (explored throughout this book) to choose appropriate ingredients. Earthy options include root vegetables, legumes, and whole grains. Watery choices encompass broths, fruits, and leafy greens.

4. Cooking Techniques Aligned with Elements: Remember, cooking methods can also influence the elemental properties of a dish. Earthy techniques like slow cooking and roasting enhance the grounding qualities of ingredients. Watery methods like simmering and poaching emphasize the gentle, nourishing nature of water-based dishes.

5. Experiment and Listen: This is a personalized approach. Experiment with different elemental combinations and observe how they affect you. Be mindful of your body's response and adjust your meals accordingly.

Elemental diets are not meant to be restrictive but rather a guiding principle. You can incorporate these concepts into your everyday meals. Perhaps a light and airy salad for lunch (air) followed by a comforting lentil soup (earth) for dinner. Remember, the beauty lies in the exploration and the journey towards a more balanced you through the wisdom of the elements.

The Five Elements: A Symphony of Flavors and Techniques

THE MAGIC OF ELEMENTAL cooking lies in understanding the unique characteristics of each element – earth, air, fire, water, and spirit – and how they translate into the culinary experience. Let's delve into the essence of each element, exploring their associated flavors, and the cooking methods that best bring forth their power.

Earth: The Grounding Embrace

- **Characteristics:** Stability, solidity, nourishment.
- **Flavors:** Sweet, savory, nutty.
- **Cooking Methods:** Roasting, slow cooking, braising, baking.

Earth is the foundation, the comforting embrace that nourishes and grounds. Earthy flavors are often sweet and savory, with hints of nuttiness. Think of the caramelized sweetness of roasted root vegetables, the rich earthiness of a lentil stew, or the comforting warmth of a freshly baked loaf of bread.

Cooking methods that celebrate earth involve slow transformations. Roasting vegetables brings out their natural sweetness, while slow cooking stews allows flavors to meld and meld. The warmth of the oven is earth's domain, where ingredients are nurtured and transformed into nourishing dishes.

Air: Lightness and Upliftment

- **Characteristics:** Lightness, delicacy, fleeting joy.

- **Flavors:** Delicate, sweet, refreshing.
- **Cooking Methods:** Whipping, folding, quick cooking, steaming.

Air embodies the essence of lightness and ephemeral joy. Airy flavors are delicate and often sweet, with a refreshing quality. Imagine the pillowy lightness of a meringue, the fluffy texture of a soufflé, or the vibrant freshness of a summer salad.

Cooking techniques that respect air's essence are quick and gentle. Whipping egg whites incorporates air, creating airy mousses and soufflés. Folding ingredients maintains delicate textures, while steaming preserves the vibrant colors and freshness of vegetables.

Fire: Transformation and Passion

- **Characteristics:** Transformation, passion, intensity.
- **Flavors:** Bold, spicy, smoky.
- **Cooking Methods:** Grilling, searing, stir-frying, smoking.

Fire is the element of transformation, where ingredients undergo dramatic changes. Fiery flavors are bold and intense, often with a touch of heat or smokiness. Think of the searing sear of a perfectly grilled steak, the vibrant spice of a stir-fry, or the smoky depth of roasted peppers.

Cooking techniques that unleash fire's power involve high heat and direct contact. Grilling creates a beautiful char and smoky flavor, while searing locks in juices and delivers a satisfying crust. Stir-frying is a dance with fire, creating dishes that are both quick and intensely flavored.

Water: Adaptability and Flow

- **Characteristics:** Adaptability, nurturing, flow.
- **Flavors:** Subtle, delicate, sometimes slightly salty.
- **Cooking Methods:** Poaching, simmering, braising, steaming.

Water is the essence of adaptability and flow. Watery flavors are often subtle and delicate, sometimes with a hint of salinity. Imagine the comforting warmth of a bowl of broth, the silky texture of poached salmon, or the vibrant freshness of steamed vegetables.

Cooking techniques that celebrate water involve gentle simmering and slow transformations. Poaching allows delicate ingredients to cook gently, while simmering broths extract deep flavors from bones and vegetables. Steaming preserves the delicate textures and vibrant colors of vegetables.

Spirit: Creativity and Intuition

- **Characteristics:** Creativity, intuition, boundless potential.
- **Flavors:** Unexpected, surprising, a symphony of all elements.
- **Cooking Methods:** Unconventional techniques, playful presentations.

Spirit is the essence of boundless creativity and intuition. It's about pushing boundaries and expressing your unique culinary voice. There are no specific flavors associated with spirit, as it encompasses the entire spectrum of culinary possibilities.

Spirit thrives on experimentation. Explore unconventional techniques like molecular gastronomy, create playful and artistic presentations, or surprise your palate with unexpected flavor combinations. This is where your culinary journey takes flight, guided by your own creativity and intuition.

By understanding the essence of each element and their corresponding techniques and flavors, you unlock a whole new world of culinary possibilities. As you delve deeper into this book, we'll explore these elements further, crafting dishes that are not only delicious but also resonate with the unique symphony of the five elements.

Benefits of Elemental Cooking: A Journey Beyond the Plate

ELEMENTAL COOKING IS more than just a collection of recipes. It's a philosophy, a way of approaching food that unlocks a world of benefits that extend far beyond the satisfaction of a delicious meal. Let's explore how this unique approach can enrich your culinary journey.

1. Unlocking Creativity: Elemental cooking breaks free from rigid recipes and encourages experimentation. By understanding the essence of each element and their associated techniques, you become a culinary alchemist, transforming ingredients into dishes that reflect your own creativity. Whether it's incorporating unexpected flavor combinations (fire and air) or creating visually stunning presentations (spirit), unleashing your inner culinary artist is a key element of the journey.

2. Deepening Appreciation for Food: Elemental cooking fosters a deeper connection with the ingredients on your plate. You begin to appreciate the inherent qualities of each element – the grounding comfort of earth, the refreshing lightness of air, the transformative heat of fire, the life-giving essence of water. This newfound awareness elevates the simple act of eating into a mindful and enriching experience.

3. Promoting Well-being: The five elements are not just culinary concepts, but also resonate with Traditional Chinese Medicine (TCM) principles. By understanding the connection between elements and your internal balance, you can create meals that not only nourish your body but also support your overall well-being. Craving energy (water)? Craft a hydrating fruit salad. Feeling sluggish (earth)? Opt for a grounding lentil soup. Elemental cooking empowers you to make conscious choices about food that contribute to a balanced and healthy you.

4. A Celebration of the Seasons: Each element has a natural affinity with specific seasons. Earthier ingredients like root vegetables and squash are abundant in fall, while lighter, airier dishes like salads and fruit crisps grace our tables in summer. By aligning your cooking with the seasons, you not only embrace fresh, local ingredients but also create a deeper connection with nature's rhythms.

5. A Shared Experience: Elemental cooking fosters connection. When you gather around a table filled with dishes that embody the elements, you create a shared experience that transcends mere sustenance. The conversation flows, fueled by the vibrancy of colors, textures, and flavors. It becomes a celebration of creativity, connection, and the timeless magic of food.

Elemental cooking is an invitation to explore, experiment, and connect. It's a journey that takes you beyond the recipe page, fostering a deeper appreciation for food, creativity, and your own well-being. So, preheat your oven, embrace the elements, and embark on a culinary adventure that will transform the way you cook, eat, and experience the world around you.

Part 1: Earth (10 Recipes)

Essence of Earth:

Delve into the comforting embrace of earth. This element embodies stability, solidity, and nourishment. Earthy flavors are often sweet, savory, and nutty, evoking a sense of grounding and satisfaction. Imagine the caramelized sweetness of roasted vegetables, the rich earthiness of a lentil stew, or the comforting warmth of a freshly baked loaf of bread.

Cooking with Earth:

Techniques that celebrate earth involve slow transformations, coaxing out the inherent sweetness and depth of flavor from ingredients. Here, we explore methods that perfectly showcase the essence of earth:

● **Roasting:** Roasting vegetables in the oven brings out their natural sugars, creating caramelized sweetness and a satisfying tenderness. Think roasted root vegetables, butternut squash, or Brussels sprouts.

● **Root Vegetable Usage:** Root vegetables like carrots, potatoes, and turnips are quintessential earth ingredients. They offer a natural sweetness and grounding texture, perfect for roasting, mashing, or incorporating into stews and soups.

● **Slow Cooking:** Low and slow cooking allows flavors to meld and develop, creating rich and comforting dishes. Earthy slow-cooked meals include stews, braises, and long-simmered soups, perfect for cooler weather.

● **Baking:** The gentle heat of the oven nurtures and transforms ingredients, creating comforting baked dishes like whole roasted chicken, savory pies and tarts, and crusty breads.

These techniques, along with the following recipes, will guide you on your exploration of earth's culinary essence. Get ready to create dishes that nourish your body and soul.

Roasted Root Vegetables with Herb Crust (Earthen Delight)

THIS DISH IS A CELEBRATION of earth's essence. Roasting brings out the inherent sweetness of the root vegetables, while the herb crust adds a layer of savory goodness. It's a nourishing and grounding dish, perfect for a comforting meal.

Ingredients:

- 1 pound (454 g) assorted root vegetables (carrots, parsnips, potatoes, turnips, sweet potatoes - peeled and cut into 1-inch cubes)
- 2 tablespoons (30 ml) olive oil
- 1/2 teaspoon dried thyme
- 1/4 teaspoon dried rosemary
- 1/4 teaspoon dried sage (or 1 tablespoon fresh, chopped)
- 1/2 cup (60 g) fresh breadcrumbs (gluten-free option in Tips)
- 1/4 cup (25 g) grated Parmesan cheese (vegan option in Tips)

- Salt and freshly ground black pepper, to taste

Fiery Variation (Optional):

- 1/4 teaspoon red pepper flakes

Instructions:

1. Preheat your oven to 425°F (220°C). Line a baking sheet with parchment paper.
2. In a large bowl, toss the cubed root vegetables with olive oil, thyme, rosemary, and sage. Season generously with salt and pepper.
3. Spread the vegetables in a single layer on the prepared baking sheet.
4. In a small bowl, combine the breadcrumbs, Parmesan cheese (or vegan alternative), and a pinch of salt. If using the fiery variation, add the red pepper flakes here.
5. Sprinkle the herb crust mixture evenly over the vegetables.
6. Roast for 30-40 minutes, or until the vegetables are tender and the crust is golden brown.
7. Remove from the oven and let cool slightly before serving.

Tips:

- **Gluten-Free Crust:** Use gluten-free breadcrumbs or chopped nuts (almonds, pecans, walnuts) as a substitute.
- **Vegan Crust:** Replace the Parmesan cheese with nutritional yeast or a vegan cheese alternative.
- **Herb Substitutions:** Don't have fresh herbs? Use 1 teaspoon dried herbs in total, adjusting the ratio of thyme, rosemary, and sage to your preference.
- **Sweet Touch:** Drizzle the vegetables with a tablespoon of honey or maple syrup before roasting for a touch of sweetness.
- **Leftovers Delight:** These roasted vegetables are delicious served cold the next day in salads or wraps.

Allergy/Diet Information:

This recipe can be easily adapted to be gluten-free, vegan, and nut-free (depending on the chosen breadcrumb substitute). Be sure to check the ingredients label of your chosen breadcrumbs and Parmesan cheese (or substitute) for potential allergens.

Earthy Connection:

This dish embodies the grounding and nourishing qualities of the earth element. The root vegetables represent stability and sustenance, while the herbs add a touch of vitality. Enjoying this dish fosters a sense of connection to the earth's bounty and its inherent ability to nourish and comfort.

Lentil and Mushroom Stew (Earthy Comfort with a Watery Touch)

THIS HEARTY STEW EMBODIES the comforting embrace of earth, with earthy lentils and savory mushrooms simmered in a rich broth. The optional variation adds a touch of the water element with fresh herbs, fostering a sense of balance and vitality.

Ingredients:

- 1 tablespoon (15 ml) olive oil
- 1 medium onion, diced
- 2 cloves garlic, minced
- 1 pound (454 g) assorted mushrooms (cremini, portobello, shiitake - sliced)
- 1 cup (230 g) brown lentils, rinsed
- 4 cups (960 ml) vegetable broth
- 1 (14.5 oz/414 ml) can diced tomatoes, undrained
- 1 tablespoon tomato paste

- 1 teaspoon dried thyme
- 1/2 teaspoon dried rosemary
- Salt and freshly ground black pepper, to taste

Watery Variation (Optional):
- 1/4 cup (packed) fresh parsley, chopped
- 1/4 cup (packed) fresh dill, chopped

Instructions:

1. Heat olive oil in a large Dutch oven or pot over medium heat. Add the onion and cook, stirring occasionally, until softened (about 5 minutes).
2. Add the garlic and cook for an additional minute, until fragrant.
3. Increase the heat to medium-high and add the mushrooms. Cook, stirring occasionally, until the mushrooms are browned and softened (about 5-7 minutes).
4. Stir in the lentils, vegetable broth, diced tomatoes, tomato paste, thyme, and rosemary. Season generously with salt and pepper.
5. Bring to a boil, then reduce heat to low, cover, and simmer for 30-35 minutes, or until the lentils are tender and the stew has thickened.
6. If using the watery variation, stir in the fresh parsley and dill just before serving.

Tips:

- **Spruce it Up:** For a richer flavor, add a tablespoon of soy sauce or a splash of Worcestershire sauce along with the broth.
- **Creamy Twist:** After the lentils are cooked, remove about 1 cup of the stew and blend it with an immersion blender until smooth. Return the puree to the pot and stir to combine for a creamier texture.
- **Leftovers:** This stew reheats beautifully and tastes even better the next day.
- **Don't have Brown Lentils?** Green lentils can be substituted with a slightly shorter cooking time (around 20-25 minutes).

Allergy/Diet Information:

This recipe is naturally vegan and gluten-free. Be sure to check the ingredients label of your vegetable broth for potential allergens.

Earthy and Watery Harmony:

This stew celebrates the connection between earth and water elements. The lentils and mushrooms provide grounding earthiness, while the broth and optional fresh herbs add a touch of the water element's nurturing essence. This harmonious balance creates a comforting and nourishing dish.

Potato and Goat Cheese Gratin (Earthy and Creamy Delight)

THIS DISH IS A SYMPHONY of earth and air, celebrating the comforting richness of potatoes and the delicate tang of goat cheese. The creamy sauce and crispy topping create a textural contrast that's both satisfying and delightful.

Ingredients:

- 2 pounds (907 g) Yukon Gold potatoes (peeled and thinly sliced - about 1/8 inch thick)
- 3 tablespoons (45 ml) unsalted butter
- 3 cloves garlic, minced
- 1/4 cup (60 g) all-purpose flour (gluten-free option in Tips)
- 2 cups (480 ml) whole milk (dairy-free option in Tips)
- 1 cup (240 ml) heavy cream (dairy-free option in Tips)
- 1/2 teaspoon ground nutmeg
- 1 teaspoon dried thyme
- Salt and freshly ground black pepper, to taste

- 4 ounces (113 g) goat cheese, crumbled
- 1/4 cup (40 g) grated Parmesan cheese

Instructions:

1. Preheat oven to 400°F (200°C). Lightly grease a 9x13 inch (23x33 cm) baking dish.
2. In a large pot of boiling salted water, cook the potato slices for 3-4 minutes, or until just tender. Drain well and set aside.
3. In a saucepan over medium heat, melt the butter. Add the garlic and cook for 30 seconds, until fragrant.
4. Whisk in the flour and cook for 1 minute, stirring constantly.
5. Slowly whisk in the milk and cream, whisking constantly until the mixture thickens and becomes smooth.
6. Bring to a simmer and cook for 2-3 minutes, or until slightly thickened. Season with nutmeg, thyme, salt, and pepper.
7. Remove from the heat and stir in the crumbled goat cheese until melted and incorporated.
8. In a single layer, spread half of the cooked potato slices in the prepared baking dish. Pour half of the cheese sauce over the potatoes. Repeat with the remaining potatoes and cheese sauce.
9. Sprinkle the top with Parmesan cheese.
10. Bake for 30-35 minutes, or until the gratin is bubbly and the top is golden brown.
11. Let cool slightly before serving.

Tips:

- **Gluten-Free Option:** Substitute all-purpose flour with a gluten-free flour blend that works well for baking.
- **Dairy-Free Option:** Use dairy-free milk and cream alternatives. Choose varieties that are suitable for baking and thickening. Opt for a dairy-free goat cheese alternative or omit it altogether for a vegan version.
- **Creamy Boost:** For an extra decadent dish, stir in 1/4 cup grated Gruyère cheese with the goat cheese.
- **Leftovers:** This gratin reheats well. Cover with foil and bake at 350°F (175°C) for 20-25 minutes, or until warmed through.

Allergy/Diet Information:

This recipe can be adapted to be gluten-free and dairy-free with the suggested substitutions. Be sure to check the ingredients label of your chosen substitutes for potential allergens.

Earthy and Airy Balance:

This gratin embodies the harmonious dance between earth and air elements. The potatoes represent the comforting solidity of earth, while the creamy sauce and airy texture introduce a touch of air's lightness. The result is a dish that's both satisfying and delightful.

Beef Bourguignon (Earthy Elegance with a Fiery Kiss)

THIS CLASSIC FRENCH dish is a celebration of earth's bounty and fire's transformative power. Rich beef is slowly braised in a robust red wine sauce, infused with earthy vegetables and aromatics. A touch of fire, optional but delightful, adds depth and complexity.

Ingredients:

- 1 tablespoon (15 ml) olive oil
- 1 pound (454 g) beef chuck roast, cut into 1-inch cubes
- 10 slices (150 g) thick-cut bacon, diced
- 1 large onion, diced
- 2 carrots, peeled and diced
- 2 celery stalks, diced
- 4 cloves garlic, minced
- 1 tablespoon (10 g) tomato paste

- 1 bottle (750 ml) full-bodied red wine (such as Burgundy, Pinot Noir, or Merlot)
- 2 cups (480 ml) beef broth
- 1 bay leaf
- 4 sprigs fresh thyme (or 1 teaspoon dried thyme)
- 1/2 teaspoon dried rosemary
- Salt and freshly ground black pepper, to taste
- Optional - Fiery Touch:

  ○ 1/4 teaspoon red pepper flakes

Instructions:

1. Preheat oven to 325°F (165°C).
2. Heat olive oil in a large Dutch oven or heavy-bottomed pot over medium-high heat. Season the beef cubes generously with salt and pepper. Sear the beef in batches, working in a single layer and avoiding overcrowding the pot. Cook until browned on all sides. Remove the browned beef and set aside.
3. Add the bacon to the pot and cook over medium heat until browned and crispy. Remove the bacon with a slotted spoon and set aside. Leave some of the bacon fat in the pot for added flavor.
4. Reduce the heat to medium-low and add the onion, carrots, and celery. Cook, stirring occasionally, until softened and translucent (about 5-7 minutes).
5. Stir in the garlic and cook for an additional minute, until fragrant.
6. Add the tomato paste and cook for another minute, stirring constantly, to allow the tomato paste to release its flavor.
7. Pour in the red wine, scraping up any browned bits from the bottom of the pot. Bring to a simmer and cook for 5 minutes, allowing the alcohol to slightly reduce.
8. Return the browned beef and any accumulated juices to the pot. Add the beef broth, bay leaf, thyme, and rosemary. Season with salt and pepper to taste.
9. (Optional - Fiery Touch) If you prefer a touch of heat, add the red pepper flakes at this point.
10. Bring to a boil, then cover and transfer the pot to the preheated oven. Braise for 2-2 ½ hours, or until the beef is very tender and falling apart.
11. Remove the pot from the oven and discard the bay leaf. Stir in the reserved cooked bacon.
12. Serve hot with mashed potatoes, crusty bread, or your favorite side dish.

Tips:

- **Marinating Magic:** For an extra layer of flavor, marinate the beef cubes in red wine, herbs, and aromatics overnight before searing.
- **Mushroom Medley:** Add 1 pound (454 g) sliced mushrooms (cremini, portobello, or a mix) along with the vegetables for an earthy and savory twist.
- **Thicken the Sauce:** If you prefer a thicker sauce, after removing the beef and vegetables, whisk together 1 tablespoon cornstarch with 2 tablespoons of cold water to form a slurry. Gradually whisk the slurry into the simmering sauce until thickened to your desired consistency.
- **Leftovers Delight:** This dish tastes even better the next day. The flavors will have further developed, and the leftovers reheat beautifully.

Allergy/Diet Information:

This recipe is not gluten-free or vegetarian due to the beef and bacon. However, you can explore substitutions for a more dietary-friendly version. Consider using a plant-based meat substitute for the beef and omitting the bacon. Opt for a full-bodied red wine that is suitable for vegans when making substitutions.

Earthy and Fiery Symphony:

Beef Bourguignon embodies the harmonious interplay of earth and fire elements. The beef and vegetables represent the grounding essence of earth, while the red wine and optional red pepper flakes introduce a touch of fire's transformative heat. This combination results in a rich, complex, and deeply satisfying dish.

Whole Roasted Chicken with Root Vegetables (Earthy Feast from the Oven)

THIS DISH IS A CELEBRATION of earth's bounty. A succulent whole chicken roasts to golden perfection, nestled amongst a colorful medley of root vegetables. The slow roasting process coaxes out the natural sweetness of the vegetables and infuses them with the savory essence of the chicken.

Ingredients:

- 1 whole chicken (4-5 pounds/1.8-2.3 kg)
- 1 tablespoon (15 ml) olive oil
- 1 lemon, halved
- 1 head garlic, cut in half crosswise
- 1 tablespoon fresh thyme, chopped (or 1 teaspoon dried)
- 1 tablespoon fresh rosemary, chopped (or 1 teaspoon dried)
- Kosher salt and freshly ground black pepper
- 1 pound (454 g) assorted root vegetables (such as carrots, potatoes, parsnips, turnips, sweet potatoes) - peeled and cut into 1-inch cubes

Instructions:

1. Preheat oven to 425°F (220°C). Lightly grease a large roasting pan.
2. Pat the chicken dry with paper towels. Season the cavity generously with salt and pepper. Stuff the cavity with the lemon halves and garlic.
3. Tie the chicken legs together with kitchen twine (optional). Rub the outside of the chicken with olive oil and season generously with salt and pepper.
4. Arrange the cubed root vegetables in a single layer around the chicken in the prepared roasting pan. Scatter the herbs over the vegetables.
5. Place the chicken on top of the vegetables, breast side up.
6. Roast for 1 hour and 15 minutes, or until the chicken is golden brown and cooked through. The internal temperature of the thickest part of the thigh should reach 165°F (74°C). Baste the chicken and vegetables with the pan juices occasionally throughout roasting.
7. If the vegetables start to brown too quickly, tent the pan loosely with foil during the last 20 minutes of roasting.
8. Remove from the oven and let the chicken rest for 10-15 minutes before carving.

Tips:

- **Flavor Boost:** Stuff the cavity with additional aromatics like chopped onion, orange wedges, or a few sprigs of fresh sage.
- **Crispy Skin:** To ensure crispy skin, pat the chicken dry thoroughly before seasoning and roasting. During the last 30 minutes of roasting, increase the oven temperature to 450°F (230°C) to crisp the skin.
- **Roasting Time Variation:** Roasting time may vary slightly depending on the size of the chicken. Use a meat thermometer to ensure the chicken is cooked through.
- **Leftover Magic:** Leftover roasted chicken and vegetables can be used in a variety of dishes, such as salads, sandwiches, or chicken pot pie.

Allergy/Diet Information:

This recipe is naturally gluten-free. However, be sure to check the ingredients label of your chosen olive oil for potential allergens. This recipe can be adapted to be dairy-free by omitting the butter (if used for basting).

Earthy Celebration:

This dish is a testament to the abundance of earth. The whole chicken represents a source of sustenance, while the root vegetables offer a vibrant display of earthy flavors and textures. Roasting brings out the natural sweetness of the vegetables and infuses them with the savory essence of the chicken, creating a harmonious and nourishing meal.

Earthy Lentil Soup: A Celebration of the Ground

THIS HEARTY LENTIL soup embodies the grounding energy of Earth. It's a simple yet soul-satisfying dish, bursting with earthy flavors and packed with protein and fiber.

Ingredients:

- 2 tablespoons olive oil
- 1 medium yellow onion, diced (about 1 cup)
- 2 carrots, diced (about 1 cup)
- 2 celery stalks, diced (about 1 cup)
- 3 cloves garlic, minced
- 1 teaspoon dried thyme
- 1/2 teaspoon ground cumin
- 1/4 teaspoon ground coriander
- Pinch of red pepper flakes (optional)

- 1 (14.5-ounce) can diced tomatoes, undrained
- 4 cups vegetable broth
- 1 cup green lentils, rinsed
- 1 cup chopped baby potatoes (optional)
- 4 cups chopped kale or spinach
- Salt and freshly ground black pepper, to taste
- Fresh herbs (optional): parsley, cilantro, or dill

Conversions:

- 1 tablespoon = 15 ml
- 1 cup = 240 ml (US customary) or 250 ml (metric)
- 1 medium clove garlic = 5 grams

Tips:

- For a richer flavor, you can substitute chicken broth for vegetable broth.
- If you don't have fresh herbs, 1 teaspoon dried parsley, cilantro, or dill can be used in their place.
- To make the soup thicker, mash some of the cooked lentils against the side of the pot with a fork.
- This soup is even more delicious the next day, as the flavors have a chance to meld further.

Allergy/Diet Differences:

- **Vegan:** This recipe is naturally vegan. Ensure the vegetable broth you use is certified vegan.
- **Gluten-free:** This recipe is naturally gluten-free.
- **Dairy-free:** This recipe is naturally dairy-free.

Instructions:

1. Heat olive oil in a large pot or Dutch oven over medium heat. Add the onion, carrots, and celery and cook, stirring occasionally, until softened, about 5 minutes.
2. Stir in the garlic, thyme, cumin, coriander, and red pepper flakes (if using) and cook for another minute, until fragrant.
3. Add the diced tomatoes, vegetable broth, lentils, and potatoes (if using). Bring to a boil, then reduce heat, cover, and simmer for 20-25 minutes, or until the lentils are tender.
4. Stir in the kale or spinach and cook for an additional 2-3 minutes, or until wilted.
5. Season with salt and black pepper to taste.
6. Serve hot, garnished with fresh herbs (optional).

Additional Notes:

- This recipe is a wonderful base for customization. Feel free to add other vegetables of your choice, such as mushrooms, zucchini, or bell peppers.
- You can also experiment with different herbs and spices. Smoked paprika, turmeric, or a pinch of cayenne pepper would all be delicious additions.
- Leftovers can be stored in an airtight container in the refrigerator for up to 4 days.

Enjoy this taste of the Earth's bounty!

Butternut Squash Risotto: A Creamy Ode to Autumn

THIS DECADENT BUTTERNUT squash risotto captures the essence of Fire's warmth and Earth's grounding energy. The creamy rice envelops the sweet, caramelized squash, creating a dish that's both comforting and elegant.

Ingredients:

- 3 tablespoons olive oil, divided
- 1 medium yellow onion, diced (about 1 cup)
- 1/2 teaspoon sea salt, plus more to taste
- Freshly ground black pepper
- 1 (medium) butternut squash (about 1.5 pounds), peeled, seeded, and cubed (about 3 cups)
- 2 garlic cloves, minced
- 1 teaspoon chopped fresh thyme (or 1/2 teaspoon dried thyme)
- 1 cup Arborio rice
- ½ cup dry white wine (optional)

- 4 cups vegetable broth, warmed
- ½ cup grated Parmesan cheese
- 1 tablespoon unsalted butter (optional)
- Chopped fresh sage or parsley, for garnish (optional)

Conversions:

- 1 tablespoon = 15 ml
- 1 cup = 240 ml (US customary) or 250 ml (metric)
- 1 medium clove garlic = 5 grams

Tips:

- Roasting the squash beforehand intensifies its sweetness and flavor. If short on time, you can skip this step and simply sauté the cubed squash in the pan with the onions. However, roasting is highly recommended for the best results.
- To roast the squash, preheat your oven to 400°F (200°C). Toss the cubed squash with 1 tablespoon olive oil, salt, and pepper. Spread on a baking sheet and roast for 20-25 minutes, or until tender and slightly caramelized.
- For a richer flavor, substitute chicken broth for vegetable broth.
- Ensure the broth is simmering before adding it to the rice, a ladleful at a time. This gradual addition allows the rice to absorb the flavorful liquid, resulting in a creamy texture.
- If you prefer a vegan option, omit the butter and use a vegan Parmesan cheese substitute.

Allergy/Diet Differences:

- **Vegetarian:** This recipe is naturally vegetarian.
- **Gluten-free:** This recipe is naturally gluten-free, provided the vegetable broth used is certified gluten-free.
- **Dairy-free:** To make this recipe dairy-free, omit the butter and Parmesan cheese. You can use a vegan Parmesan cheese substitute or a sprinkle of nutritional yeast for a cheesy flavor.

Instructions:

1. Heat 1 tablespoon olive oil in a large pot or Dutch oven over medium heat. Add the onion and cook, stirring occasionally, until softened and translucent, about 5 minutes. Season with salt and pepper.
2. If roasting the squash, follow the tip above. If not roasting, add the cubed squash to the pot with the onions and cook for 5-7 minutes, stirring occasionally, until slightly softened.
3. Stir in the garlic and thyme and cook for an additional minute, until fragrant.
4. Add the Arborio rice and cook, stirring constantly, for 1 minute to coat the rice with the oil.
5. Pour in the white wine (if using) and cook, stirring frequently, until the wine is absorbed.
6. Begin adding the warmed vegetable broth, one ladleful at a time, stirring constantly after each addition and allowing the rice to absorb the liquid before adding more broth. Continue adding broth until the rice is cooked through, but still has a slight bite, about 18-20 minutes. The risotto should be creamy and not soupy.
7. Once the rice is cooked, stir in the Parmesan cheese and butter (if using). Season with additional salt and pepper to taste.
8. Serve immediately, garnished with fresh sage or parsley (optional).

Additional Notes:

- This risotto is a delicious accompaniment to roasted chicken, grilled fish, or a simple green salad.
- Leftovers can be stored in an airtight container in the refrigerator for up to 3 days. Reheat gently over low heat, adding a splash of broth or water if needed to thin out the consistency.

Savor this dish, a delightful marriage of Fire's warmth and Earth's bounty.

Baked Apples with Cinnamon and Nuts: An Airy Dance with Autumn's Bounty

THIS RECIPE CELEBRATES the airy essence of Air with light and fluffy baked apples, while the warming cinnamon and crunchy nuts pay homage to Earth's grounding energy. It's a simple yet delightful dessert perfect for a cozy autumn evening.

Ingredients:
- 4 apples (such as Granny Smith, Honeycrisp, or Gala)
- 2 tablespoons unsalted butter, softened
- 1/4 cup packed light brown sugar
- 1/2 teaspoon ground cinnamon
- 1/4 teaspoon ground nutmeg (optional)
- 1/2 cup chopped nuts (such as walnuts, pecans, or almonds)
- 1/4 cup raisins or chopped dried cranberries (optional)
- 1 tablespoon lemon juice (optional)

- Pinch of salt
- 1/4 cup water (optional)

Conversions:

- 1 tablespoon = 15 ml
- 1/4 cup = 60 ml (US customary) or 50 ml (metric)
- 1/2 teaspoon = 2.5 ml

Tips:

- Choose apples that are firm and tart, such as Granny Smith or Honeycrisp. These hold their shape well during baking.
- For a richer flavor, use dark brown sugar instead of light brown sugar.
- To prevent the apples from browning too quickly, brush the cut surfaces with lemon juice.
- If your apples are not very juicy, adding a splash of water to the baking dish will help prevent them from drying out.
- Don't overbake the apples. You want them to be tender but still hold their shape.

Allergy/Diet Differences:

- **Vegan:** To make this recipe vegan, omit the butter and use a vegan butter substitute.
- **Gluten-free:** This recipe is naturally gluten-free, provided the chosen nuts are certified gluten-free.
- **Nut-free:** For a nut-free option, omit the nuts and substitute with an additional 1/4 cup of chopped dried fruit.

Instructions:

1. Preheat oven to 375°F (190°C). Lightly grease a baking dish.
2. Core the apples, leaving the bottom intact. You can use an apple corer or a sharp paring knife.
3. In a medium bowl, cream together the softened butter, brown sugar, cinnamon, nutmeg (if using), and a pinch of salt. Stir in the chopped nuts and raisins or dried cranberries (if using).
4. Divide the filling mixture amongst the cored apples, packing it gently into the cavity.
5. Pour the water (if using) into the bottom of the baking dish.
6. Bake for 30-40 minutes, or until the apples are tender and a fork can easily pierce through them.
7. Serve warm, spooned with any drippings from the baking dish and a scoop of vanilla ice cream (optional).

Additional Notes:

- For an extra decadent touch, drizzle the baked apples with a touch of honey or maple syrup before serving.
- This recipe can be easily doubled or tripled to serve a crowd.
- Leftover baked apples can be stored in an airtight container in the refrigerator for up to 3 days. Reheat gently in the microwave or oven before serving.

Indulge in this delightful dance of Airy textures and Earthy flavors, a perfect embodiment of the autumn season.

Chocolate Babka Bread: A Swirling Symphony of Earth and Fire

THIS RECIPE WEAVES together the rich, grounding energy of Earth (cocoa, dough) with the fiery passion (chocolate filling) for a truly delightful babka bread. The spiraled layers of dough encasing a decadent chocolate filling create a textural and flavor explosion in every bite.

Ingredients:

Dough:

- 1 cup (240ml) warm milk (105°F/40°C)
- 2 1/4 teaspoons (7g) active dry yeast
- 3 tablespoons (45g) granulated sugar
- 2 large eggs, at room temperature
- 4 ½ cups (560g) all-purpose flour, plus extra for dusting
- 1 teaspoon (5g) salt
- 6 tablespoons (85g) unsalted butter, softened

Chocolate Filling:

- ½ cup (1 stick) unsalted butter
- ¾ cup (60g) unsweetened cocoa powder
- ½ cup (100g) powdered sugar
- ¼ cup (60ml) heavy cream
- 1 teaspoon (5ml) vanilla extract

Egg Wash:

- 1 large egg yolk
- 1 tablespoon (15ml) milk

Conversions:

- 1 cup = 240 ml (US customary) or 250 ml (metric)
- 1 tablespoon = 15 ml
- 1 teaspoon = 5 ml
- 1 stick of butter = 8 tablespoons or 113g

Tips:

- Ensure the milk is warm to the touch, but not hot, to activate the yeast. If the milk is too hot, it will kill the yeast and your dough will not rise.
- For richer flavor, use dark brown sugar in the dough instead of granulated sugar.
- The dough can be chilled overnight for up to 24 hours. This allows the flavors to develop further and makes the dough easier to roll out.
- When rolling out the dough, use a light dusting of flour to prevent sticking. However, be mindful of adding too much flour, as it can toughen the dough.
- To achieve even layers of chocolate filling, spread it thinly and evenly over the dough rectangle.
- If the chocolate filling becomes too soft while spreading, place the filled dough in the refrigerator for 15-20 minutes to firm up before shaping.

Allergy/Diet Differences:

- **Vegetarian:** This recipe is naturally vegetarian.
- **Egg-free:** This recipe can be adapted to be egg-free. For the dough, use a flaxseed egg substitute (1 tablespoon ground flaxseed mixed with 3 tablespoons water, let sit for 10 minutes) in place of each egg. Omit the egg wash or use a vegan milk wash.
- **Dairy-free:** To make this recipe dairy-free, use a vegan butter substitute for the dough and filling. Use a dairy-free milk alternative for the egg wash.

Instructions:

Dough:

1. In a large bowl or stand mixer fitted with a dough hook, combine the warm milk, yeast, and sugar. Let sit for 5 minutes, or until the yeast becomes foamy.
2. Stir in the eggs, then gradually add the flour and salt. Mix until a soft dough forms.
3. Knead the dough on a lightly floured surface for 5-7 minutes, or until smooth and elastic. Add more flour a tablespoon at a time if the dough is too sticky.
4. Knead in the softened butter, one tablespoon at a time, until fully incorporated.
5. Place the dough in a greased bowl, cover with plastic wrap, and let rise in a warm place for 1-2 hours, or until doubled in size.

Chocolate Filling:

1. In a small saucepan, melt the butter over medium heat.
2. In a medium bowl, whisk together the cocoa powder, powdered sugar, and heavy cream until smooth. Stir in the melted butter and vanilla extract.
3. Let the chocolate filling cool slightly before using.

Shaping and Baking:

1. Grease a 9x13 inch loaf pan. Alternatively, you can use two smaller loaf pans.
2. Punch down the risen dough and turn it out onto a lightly floured surface. Roll the dough into a large rectangle, approximately 16x20 inches.
3. Spread the chocolate filling evenly over the dough rectangle, leaving a 1-inch border around the edges.
4. Starting from a long edge, roll up the dough tightly into a log. Pinch the seam to seal.
5. Using a sharp knife, carefully cut the dough log in half lengthwise. Twist the two halves together, chocolate filling facing up.
6. Gently transfer the twisted dough to the prepared loaf pan, tucking the ends underneath. Cover loosely with plastic wrap and let rise again in a warm place for 1-2 hours, or until doubled in size.
7. Preheat oven to 350°F (175°C).
8. In a small bowl, whisk together the egg yolk and milk for the egg wash. Brush the top of the risen dough with the egg wash.
9. Bake for 35-40 minutes, or until golden brown.
10. Let the babka cool in the pan for 10 minutes before transferring to a wire rack to cool completely.

Tips:
- For a richer golden brown color, you can brush the babka with additional egg wash after 20 minutes of baking.
- Sprinkle the top of the babka with pearl sugar or chopped nuts before baking for an extra decorative touch.
- This babka bread is best enjoyed fresh from the oven, but can be stored at room temperature for up to 2 days or frozen for up to 3 months.

Enjoy this delightful alchemy of Earth and Fire, where the rich dough embraces the decadent chocolate filling in every swirled bite!

Spiced Carrot Cake: An Earthy Celebration with a Touch of Fire

THIS SPICED CARROT cake embodies the warm, grounding energy of Earth with its abundance of carrots, nuts, and spices. A hint of cinnamon, ginger, and cloves brings in the fiery spirit, making this a delightful cake perfect for any occasion.

Ingredients:

● **Dry Ingredients:**

○ 2 ¾ cups (340g) all-purpose flour

○ 1 teaspoon baking soda

○ 1 teaspoon baking powder

○ 1 teaspoon ground cinnamon

○ ½ teaspoon ground ginger

○ ¼ teaspoon ground nutmeg

○ ¼ teaspoon ground cloves

○ 1 teaspoon salt

- **Wet Ingredients:**

○ 3 large eggs, room temperature

○ 1 ½ cups (300g) granulated sugar

○ 1 cup (200g) packed light brown sugar

○ ½ cup (120ml) vegetable oil

○ 1 cup (240ml) buttermilk (or plain yogurt thinned with milk)

○ 2 teaspoons pure vanilla extract

- **Other:**

○ 3 cups (225g) grated carrots (about 4-5 medium carrots)

○ 1 cup (100g) chopped walnuts or pecans (optional)

○ ½ cup (75g) raisins (optional)

Conversions:
- 1 cup = 240 ml (US customary) or 250 ml (metric)
- 1 teaspoon = 5 ml

Tips:
- For the freshest flavor, grate the carrots yourself instead of using pre-shredded carrots.
- Ensure your eggs and buttermilk are at room temperature for even mixing.
- To sour your own milk, add 1 tablespoon of vinegar or lemon juice to 1 cup of milk and let it sit for 5 minutes before using as a buttermilk substitute.
- If you don't have buttermilk, you can use plain yogurt thinned with milk to achieve a similar consistency.
- Toasting the nuts adds depth of flavor. Spread the chopped nuts on a baking sheet and toast in a preheated oven at 350°F (175°C) for 5-7 minutes, stirring occasionally, until fragrant.
- Don't overmix the batter once you add the dry ingredients to the wet ingredients. A few lumps are perfectly fine.

Allergy/Diet Differences:
- **Vegetarian:** This recipe is naturally vegetarian.
- **Vegan:** This recipe can be adapted to be vegan. Use a flaxseed egg substitute (1 tablespoon ground flaxseed mixed with 3 tablespoons water, let sit for 10 minutes) in place of each egg. Use a vegan yogurt or buttermilk substitute and vegan butter.
- **Gluten-free:** To make this recipe gluten-free, use a gluten-free flour blend that is certified to substitute for all-purpose flour in a 1:1 ratio.
- **Nut-free:** Omit the nuts for a nut-free option. You can add an extra ½ cup of raisins or chopped dried fruit if desired.

Instructions:

1. Preheat oven to 350°F (175°C) and grease two 9-inch round cake pans. Line the bottoms with parchment paper for easier removal.
2. In a large bowl, whisk together the flour, baking soda, baking powder, spices, and salt. Set aside.
3. In a separate large bowl, cream together the eggs, granulated sugar, and brown sugar until light and fluffy, about

3 minutes. Beat in the oil, buttermilk, and vanilla extract until well combined.

4. Gradually add the dry ingredients to the wet ingredients, mixing until just combined. Do not overmix.
5. Fold in the grated carrots, toasted nuts (if using), and raisins (if using).
6. Divide the batter evenly between the prepared cake pans.
7. Bake for 30-35 minutes, or until a toothpick inserted into the center comes out clean.
8. Let the cakes cool in the pans for 10 minutes before transferring them to a wire rack to cool completely.

Frosting (Optional):

This cake pairs beautifully with a variety of frostings. Here are a few suggestions:

- Cream cheese frosting
- Whipped vanilla frosting
- Maple cream cheese frosting

Enjoy this delightful fusion of Earth's comforting flavors and a touch of Fire's warmth, perfect for any celebration!

Part 2: Air (10 Recipes)

Essence of Air:

Air, the element of freedom and inspiration, is all about lightness, movement, and refreshing energy. It embodies the feeling of a gentle breeze, the billowing of clouds, and the weightless joy of laughter. In the kitchen, Air translates to dishes that are light and airy in texture, often utilizing quick cooking methods and incorporating whipped or foamy elements.

Cooking with Air:

To capture the essence of Air in your cooking, focus on techniques that elevate and aerate ingredients. Here are some key methods to explore:

● **Whipping and Whisking:** Air is incorporated into cream, egg whites, and batters through vigorous whisking, creating light and fluffy textures. Think soufflés, meringues, angel food cake, and whipped cream.

● **Quick Cooking:** Air encourages quick methods that preserve the delicate nature of ingredients. Steaming, stir-frying, and quick roasting are ideal for vegetables and seafood.

● **Leavening:** Baking powders and yeasts create air pockets within doughs and batters, resulting in fluffy breads, cakes, and pastries.

● **Airy Textures:** Embrace ingredients that are naturally light and airy, like soufflés, mousses, foams, and meringues.

The following ten recipes will guide you on a delicious exploration of Air's essence in the kitchen. Prepare to be uplifted and inspired by the delightful textures and refreshing flavors!

Soufflés: A Symphony of Air and Fire (Meat, Cheese, Chocolate, or Vegetable)

THE SOUFFLÉ, A CULINARY marvel, embodies the essence of Air in its most elegant form. Light and airy as a cloud, yet boasting complex flavors, it's a dish that never fails to impress. This recipe provides a master base for creating savory or sweet soufflés, allowing you to explore the versatility of Air.

Ingredients (Base recipe):

- ½ cup (1 stick) unsalted butter
- ¼ cup (30g) all-purpose flour
- 1 ¾ cups (420ml) milk, warmed
- Pinch of salt
- Pinch of freshly ground black pepper
- 4 large eggs, separated
- ¼ teaspoon cream of tartar

Conversions:

- 1 cup = 240 ml (US customary) or 250 ml (metric)
- 1 tablespoon = 15 ml
- 1 teaspoon = 5 ml
- 1 stick of butter = 8 tablespoons or 113g

Tips:

- Use high-quality ingredients for the best results. Fresh, room temperature eggs are essential for achieving proper volume.
- Separate the eggs carefully, ensuring no yolk goes into the whites. Even a small amount of yolk can prevent the whites from whipping properly.
- When whisking the egg whites, start on low speed and gradually increase to high speed. Soft peaks will form first, followed by stiff peaks. You want the whites to be billowy and hold their shape when the whisk is lifted.
- Don't overmix the batter once you fold in the egg whites. A few streaks of white are okay. Overmixing will deflate the soufflé.
- A preheated oven is crucial. The hot oven ensures the soufflé rises quickly, setting the exterior before the interior overcooks.
- Soufflés are best enjoyed immediately after baking, as they will begin to deflate over time.

Allergy/Diet Differences:

- **Vegetarian:** For a vegetarian option, omit the meat and create a vegetable soufflé using roasted vegetables or a flavorful cheese and vegetable combination.
- **Gluten-free:** This recipe can be adapted to be gluten-free by using a certified gluten-free flour blend in place of all-purpose flour.
- **Dairy-free:** To make this recipe dairy-free, use a vegan butter substitute and a dairy-free milk alternative. Note that achieving the same level of rise may be challenging in a completely dairy-free soufflé.

Basic Steps (Choose your desired variation after this point):

1. Preheat oven to 400°F (200°C). Butter a 1-quart soufflé dish or individual ramekins.
2. Melt the butter in a medium saucepan over medium heat. Whisk in the flour and cook for 1 minute, stirring constantly.
3. Gradually whisk in the warmed milk, whisking constantly until smooth and thickened. Season with salt and pepper.
4. Remove from heat and let cool slightly.
5. Separate the egg yolks from the whites. Whisk the egg yolks into the cooled sauce mixture.
6. In a clean, grease-free bowl, whisk the egg whites with the cream of tartar until soft peaks form. Gradually increase the speed to high and continue whisking until stiff peaks form. The peaks should be firm and hold their shape when the whisk is lifted.
7. Gently fold the egg whites into the sauce mixture in 3 additions, using a rubber spatula and taking care not to deflate the whites. A few streaks of white are okay.
8. Pour the batter into the prepared soufflé dish or ramekins.
9. Bake for 25-30 minutes, or until puffed and golden brown. (Baking time may vary depending on the size of your soufflé dish or ramekins.)

Variations:

- **Meat Soufflé:** After completing step 4, fold in 1 cup of cooked, shredded meat (such as chicken, ham, or sausage) into the sauce mixture.

● **Cheese Soufflé:** After completing step 4, whisk in ½ cup of grated cheese (such as Gruyère, Parmesan, or cheddar) into the sauce mixture.

● **Chocolate Soufflé:** Omit step 4 (cheese or meat) and instead, melt 4 ounces of chopped dark chocolate with 1 tablespoon of butter in a separate bowl. Once melted and smooth, fold the chocolate mixture into the cooled sauce mixture before incorporating the egg whites.

Enjoy this delightful exploration of Air's essence! Remember, the key is to work gently and ensure your egg whites are perfectly whipped for maximum volume. Let your creativity flow and explore different flavor combinations to create your own signature soufflés!

Whipped Cream and Fruit Pavlova: A Celebration of Air and Water

THIS STUNNING DESSERT embodies the lightness of Air and the refreshing essence of Water. The crisp meringue base, billowing with soft peaks, cradles a cloud of pillowy whipped cream and a vibrant array of seasonal fruits. It's a showstopping centerpiece that's surprisingly simple to prepare.

Ingredients:
- **Meringue:**

  - 4 large egg whites, at room temperature
  - Pinch of salt
  - 1 cup (200g) superfine sugar (caster sugar)
  - 1 teaspoon cornstarch
  - 1 teaspoon white vinegar

- **Whipped Cream:**

  - 1 cup (240ml) heavy whipping cream
  - ¼ cup (60g) powdered sugar
  - 1 teaspoon vanilla extract

- **Fresh Fruit:**

  - A selection of your favorite seasonal fruits, such as berries, kiwi, stone fruits, or mango (washed and sliced)

Conversions:
- 1 cup = 240 ml (US customary) or 250 ml (metric)
- 1 tablespoon = 15 ml
- 1 teaspoon = 5 ml

Tips:
- Ensure your egg whites are at room temperature for optimal volume when whisking.
- Use a clean, grease-free bowl for whipping the egg whites. Any trace of fat or yolk can prevent them from reaching their full volume.
- Gradually add the sugar to the egg whites while whisking continuously. This ensures the sugar dissolves properly and creates a stable meringue.
- The cornstarch helps prevent the meringue from becoming too weepy.
- The white vinegar adds a touch of acidity and helps stabilize the meringue.
- Don't overbake the meringue. You want it to be crisp on the outside and slightly marshmallow-like on the inside.
- Allow the meringue to cool completely before assembling the pavlova. A warm meringue will melt the whipped cream.
- Use fresh, ripe fruit for the best flavor and visual appeal.

Allergy/Diet Differences:
- **Vegetarian:** This recipe is naturally vegetarian.
- **Vegan:** To make this recipe vegan, use a vegan whipped cream alternative made from coconut milk or cashews.
- **Gluten-free:** This recipe is naturally gluten-free.

Instructions:

Meringue:

1. Preheat oven to 200°F (95°C). Line a baking sheet with parchment paper.
2. In a clean, grease-free bowl, whisk the egg whites with a pinch of salt until soft peaks form.
3. Gradually add the superfine sugar, one tablespoon at a time, while whisking continuously on high speed.

Continue whisking until stiff peaks form and the sugar is completely dissolved. The meringue should be glossy and hold its shape when the whisk is lifted.

4. Sift the cornstarch and white vinegar over the meringue and gently fold them in with a rubber spatula until just combined.
5. Spoon the meringue mixture onto the prepared baking sheet, shaping it into a round disc, approximately 8-inch diameter. Use the back of a spoon to create a slight well in the center.
6. Bake for 1-1 ½ hours, or until the meringue is crisp on the outside and slightly soft on the inside.
7. Turn off the oven and leave the meringue to cool completely inside with the oven door slightly ajar. This helps prevent cracking.

Whipped Cream:

1. In a chilled bowl, whisk the heavy whipping cream, powdered sugar, and vanilla extract until stiff peaks form.

Assembly:

1. Once the meringue is cool, carefully transfer it to a serving plate.
2. Spoon the whipped cream into the center well of the meringue.
3. Decorate the top of the pavlova with your chosen selection of fresh fruits.
4. Serve immediately and enjoy!

Tips:

• For an extra touch of elegance, you can dust the finished pavlova with a sprinkle of powdered sugar or cocoa powder.

• Leftover meringue can be stored in an airtight container at room temperature for up to 2 days. However, the texture will soften slightly.

Embrace the airy essence and refreshing flavors of this delightful dessert, a perfect meeting point of Air and Water!

Angel Food Cake: A Heavenly Embrace of Air and Water

THIS ETHEREAL ANGEL food cake embodies the essence of Air in its purest form. Light, airy, and impossibly fluffy, it melts in your mouth with a delicate sweetness. The addition of Water, in the form of egg whites, further emphasizes the weightless texture, making this cake a true celebration of Air's uplifting spirit.

Ingredients:
- **Cake:**

  ○ 1 ½ cups (190g) cake flour (not self-rising)
  ○ 1 ½ cups (300g) granulated sugar
  ○ 1 teaspoon salt
  ○ 12 large egg whites, at room temperature
  ○ 1 teaspoon cream of tartar
  ○ 1 teaspoon vanilla extract

- ○ Pinch of almond extract (optional)

- **Powdered Sugar Glaze (Optional):**

  - ○ 1 cup (120g) powdered sugar
  - ○ 3-4 tablespoons milk
  - ○ 1 teaspoon vanilla extract

Conversions:
- 1 cup = 240 ml (US customary) or 250 ml (metric)
- 1 tablespoon = 15 ml
- 1 teaspoon = 5 ml

Tips:
- Use a scale for the most accurate measurement of cake flour. Cake flour has a lower protein content than all-purpose flour, which contributes to the cake's airy texture.
- Sift the cake flour several times to aerate it and remove any lumps.
- Separate the eggs carefully, ensuring no yolk gets into the whites. Even a small amount of yolk can prevent the whites from whipping properly.
- Allow the egg whites to come to room temperature for optimal volume when whisking.
- The cream of tartar helps stabilize the egg whites and achieve stiffer peaks.
- Gradually add the sugar to the egg whites while whisking continuously. This ensures the sugar dissolves properly and creates a stable meringue.
- Don't overmix the batter once you fold in the flour. A few streaks of flour are okay. Overmixing can deflate the air incorporated into the egg whites.
- Use an angel food cake pan, which has a center tube to promote even heat distribution and prevent the cake from collapsing in the center.
- Invert the cake pan after baking to allow the cake to cool completely without collapsing.

Allergy/Diet Differences:
- **Vegetarian:** This recipe is naturally vegetarian.
- **Vegan:** This recipe is not easily adaptable to vegan due to the reliance on egg whites for structure.
- **Gluten-free:** This recipe cannot be made gluten-free as it relies on cake flour for structure.

Instructions:

Cake:

1. Preheat oven to 350°F (175°C). Prepare an angel food cake pan by dusting it with a fine mist of nonstick baking spray.
2. In a medium bowl, whisk together the cake flour and salt. Sift the mixture three times to aerate it. Set aside.
3. In a clean, grease-free bowl, whisk the egg whites with the cream of tartar on medium speed until soft peaks form.
4. Gradually increase the speed to high and continue whisking while slowly adding the sugar, one tablespoon at a time. Continue whisking until stiff peaks form. The peaks should be firm and hold their shape when the whisk is lifted.
5. Gently fold in the vanilla extract and almond extract (if using) with a rubber spatula.
6. Sift the dry ingredients (flour mixture) into the egg white mixture in three additions, folding gently with a rubber spatula after each addition until just incorporated. Be careful not to deflate the batter.

7. Pour the batter into the prepared angel food cake pan, smoothing the top with a spatula.
8. Bake for 1 hour, or until a toothpick inserted into the center comes out clean.
9. Remove the cake from the oven and immediately invert it onto a wire rack to cool completely. This helps prevent the cake from collapsing. You can use a narrow-mouthed bottle placed in the center of the cake pan to create a stable support for inversion.

Powdered Sugar Glaze (Optional):

1. In a small bowl, whisk together the powdered sugar, milk, and vanilla extract until smooth and pourable.
2. Once the cake is cool, drizzle the glaze over the top.
3. Slice and serve.

Enjoy this ethereal delight, a testament to the lightness and sweetness of Air!

Light and Fluffy Pancakes: A Celebration of Air and Water (with Earthy Variation)

THESE DELIGHTFUL PANCAKES embody the essence of Air in every fluffy bite. Light, airy bubbles dance throughout the batter, thanks to the leavening power of baking powder and the gentle incorporation of whipped egg whites. A touch of Water, in the form of milk, brings the batter together, creating a delectable canvas for your favorite toppings. This recipe offers a classic base, with a variation to add a touch of earthiness using whole wheat flour.

Ingredients (Classic Pancakes):

● **Dry Ingredients:**

○ 1 ¾ cups (225g) all-purpose flour

○ 2 tablespoons (25g) granulated sugar

○ 2 teaspoons baking powder

○ ½ teaspoon salt

● **Wet Ingredients:**

  ○ 1 ½ cups (360ml) milk
  ○ 2 large eggs, separated
  ○ 2 tablespoons (30ml) melted butter
  ○ 1 teaspoon vanilla extract

Conversions:
● 1 cup = 240 ml (US customary) or 250 ml (metric)
● 1 tablespoon = 15 ml
● 1 teaspoon = 5 ml

Tips:
● Ensure your buttermilk or milk is at room temperature for optimal mixing.
● Separate the eggs carefully, ensuring no yolk gets into the whites. Even a small amount of yolk can prevent the whites from whipping properly.
● When whisking the egg whites, start on low speed and gradually increase to high speed. Soft peaks will form first, followed by stiff peaks. You want the whites to be billowy and hold their shape when the whisk is lifted.
● Don't overmix the batter once you fold in the egg whites. A few lumps are perfectly fine. Overmixing will deflate the air incorporated into the batter.
● Use a non-stick pan or griddle preheated over medium heat for even cooking.
● Cook the pancakes until bubbles appear on the surface and the edges begin to set. Flip the pancakes and cook for an additional minute or two, or until golden brown on both sides.

Allergy/Diet Differences:
● **Vegetarian:** This recipe is naturally vegetarian.
● **Vegan:** This recipe can be adapted to be vegan. Use a flaxseed egg substitute (1 tablespoon ground flaxseed mixed with 3 tablespoons water, let sit for 10 minutes) in place of the eggs. Use a dairy-free milk alternative.
● **Gluten-free:** For a gluten-free option, substitute the all-purpose flour with a 1:1 gluten-free baking flour blend.

Instructions (Classic Pancakes):

1. In a large bowl, whisk together the flour, sugar, baking powder, and salt.
2. In a separate bowl, whisk together the milk, egg yolks, melted butter, and vanilla extract.
3. In a clean, grease-free bowl, whisk the egg whites until stiff peaks form.
4. Gently fold the wet ingredients into the dry ingredients until just combined. Be careful not to overmix.
5. Gently fold in the whipped egg whites until just incorporated. A few streaks of white are okay.
6. Heat a non-stick pan or griddle over medium heat. Lightly grease the pan if needed.
7. Pour ¼ cup batter per pancake onto the preheated pan.
8. Cook for 2-3 minutes, or until bubbles appear on the surface and the edges begin to set.
9. Flip the pancakes and cook for an additional minute or two, or until golden brown on both sides.
10. Serve immediately with your favorite toppings, such as maple syrup, fresh fruit, whipped cream, or chocolate chips.

Earthy Variation: Whole Wheat Pancakes

For a touch of earthiness, substitute 1 cup (125g) of the all-purpose flour with 1 cup of whole wheat flour. You may need to add an additional 1-2 tablespoons of milk to achieve the desired batter consistency.

Enjoy these light and fluffy pancakes, a delightful celebration of Air! Don't forget to explore the earthy variation for a touch of grounding goodness.

Herb-Infused Salmon with Roasted Asparagus: A Symphony of Earth, Air, and Fire

THIS DISH SINGS WITH the harmonious blend of elements. The earthy notes of fresh herbs and the salmon itself are beautifully complemented by the airy lightness of roasted asparagus, all brought together by the fiery kiss of the oven. This simple yet elegant recipe allows the natural flavors to shine through, creating a satisfying and wholesome meal.

Ingredients:

- 2 salmon fillets (each about 6 ounces/170g)
- 2 tablespoons olive oil
- 1 tablespoon fresh lemon juice

- 1 teaspoon dried thyme
- ½ teaspoon dried rosemary
- ¼ teaspoon garlic powder
- Salt and freshly ground black pepper, to taste
- 1 bunch asparagus, trimmed
- 1 tablespoon melted butter (optional)

Conversions:
- 1 tablespoon = 15 ml
- 1 teaspoon = 5 ml
- 1 ounce = 28g

Tips:
- Choose fresh, firm salmon fillets for the best results.
- Allow the salmon to come to room temperature for about 30 minutes before cooking. This ensures even cooking throughout.
- Use a variety of your favorite fresh herbs, such as dill, parsley, or chives, in place of or in addition to the dried thyme and rosemary.
- Roasting the asparagus ensures even cooking and brings out its natural sweetness.
- Tossing the asparagus in a light coating of olive oil helps it brown beautifully in the oven.
- Adding melted butter to the asparagus before roasting is optional, but it adds a touch of richness.

Allergy/Diet Differences:
- **Vegetarian:** Omit the salmon and create a vegetarian dish by focusing on the roasted asparagus. You can add other roasted vegetables, such as cherry tomatoes or bell peppers, for additional variety.
- **Vegan:** This recipe can be adapted to be vegan. Use a plant-based oil instead of butter and omit the salmon. Consider marinating the tofu or tempeh in a flavorful sauce for a vegan protein option.
- **Gluten-free:** This recipe is naturally gluten-free.

Instructions:

1. Preheat oven to 400°F (200°C). Line a baking sheet with parchment paper.
2. In a small bowl, whisk together the olive oil, lemon juice, dried thyme, rosemary, garlic powder, salt, and pepper.
3. Place the salmon fillets in a shallow dish and brush them generously with the herb marinade. Let marinate for 15 minutes, or up to 30 minutes for deeper flavor.
4. Toss the asparagus with olive oil and a pinch of salt and pepper. Spread the asparagus on the prepared baking sheet in a single layer.
5. Arrange the marinated salmon fillets on top of the asparagus.
6. Bake for 15-20 minutes, or until the salmon is cooked through and flakes easily with a fork. The asparagus should be tender-crisp.
7. (Optional) Brush the asparagus with melted butter during the last few minutes of baking for added richness.
8. Serve immediately with roasted asparagus and any remaining pan juices.

Enjoy this delightful dance of elements on your plate! The earthiness of the herbs and salmon, the lightness of the asparagus, and the kiss of fire from the oven create a truly satisfying culinary experience.

Spicy Chicken Lettuce Wraps: An Earthy Symphony with a Hint of Fire

(Variation: Ignite the Flame)

THESE LETTUCE WRAPS embody the essence of Earth with their base of savory ground chicken and crisp lettuce leaves. A touch of Fire peeks through with the addition of chili peppers and spices, creating a flavor explosion in every bite. This recipe offers a classic base, with a fiery variation for those who crave an extra kick.

Ingredients (Classic Recipe):

● **Filling:**

   ○ 1 pound (450g) ground chicken
   ○ 1 tablespoon olive oil
   ○ 1 medium onion, chopped
   ○ 1 red bell pepper, chopped
   ○ 2 cloves garlic, minced
   ○ 1 teaspoon ground ginger

- 1 teaspoon chili powder
- ½ teaspoon cumin
- ¼ teaspoon smoked paprika
- Pinch of cayenne pepper (optional)
- 1/4 cup soy sauce
- 1/4 cup low-sodium chicken broth
- 1 tablespoon cornstarch
- Salt and freshly ground black pepper, to taste

- **Wraps:**

  - 1 head romaine lettuce, leaves separated and washed

  - Optional toppings: Chopped green onions, chopped cilantro, sliced avocado

Conversions:
- 1 pound = 454g
- 1 tablespoon = 15 ml
- 1 teaspoon = 5 ml

Tips:
- Lean ground chicken (around 90% lean) works best for this recipe.
- You can substitute ground turkey for chicken if desired.
- Feel free to adjust the amount of chili pepper or cayenne pepper depending on your spice preference.
- The cornstarch helps thicken the sauce slightly. Mix it with the chicken broth to create a slurry before adding it to the pan.
- Allow the cooked filling to cool slightly before assembling the lettuce wraps. Warm filling can wilt the lettuce leaves.

Allergy/Diet Differences:
- **Vegetarian:** Omit the chicken and create a vegetarian filling using crumbled tempeh or lentils. Saute the tempeh or lentils with the vegetables and adjust the seasonings accordingly.
- **Vegan:** This recipe can be adapted to be vegan. Use a plant-based ground meat alternative and a vegan soy sauce substitute.
- **Gluten-free:** This recipe is naturally gluten-free.

Instructions (Classic Recipe):

1. In a large skillet, heat olive oil over medium heat. Add the ground chicken and cook until browned, breaking it up with a spoon as it cooks.
2. Add the onion, bell pepper, and garlic to the pan and cook for 3-4 minutes, or until softened.
3. Stir in the ginger, chili powder, cumin, smoked paprika, and cayenne pepper (if using). Cook for an additional minute, allowing the spices to become fragrant.
4. Pour in the soy sauce and chicken broth. Bring to a simmer and cook for 2 minutes.
5. In a small bowl, whisk together the cornstarch and a splash of cold water to create a slurry. Add the slurry to the pan and stir continuously until the sauce thickens slightly.
6. Season with salt and pepper to taste.
7. Remove the pan from heat and allow the filling to cool slightly.

8. To assemble the wraps, place a spoonful of the chicken filling onto a romaine lettuce leaf. Top with your desired garnishes, such as chopped green onions, cilantro, or sliced avocado.

9. Serve immediately and enjoy!

Fiery Variation: Ignite the Flame with Sriracha Mayo

For those who love a kick of heat, whip up a sriracha mayo dipping sauce to accompany these lettuce wraps. Here's what you'll need:

- ¼ cup mayonnaise
- 1-2 tablespoons sriracha sauce (depending on desired spice level)
- 1 tablespoon lime juice
- Pinch of salt

Simply whisk together the mayonnaise, sriracha, lime juice, and salt in a small bowl. This adds an extra layer of fiery flavor to your lettuce wraps.

Embrace the Earthy essence of the chicken and lettuce, enlivened by a touch of Fire! Explore the classic recipe or ignite the flame with the sriracha mayo variation for a truly satisfying meal.

Summer Salad with a Light Vinaigrette: A Symphony of Earth and Water

THIS VIBRANT SUMMER salad sings with the essence of Earth and Water. Fresh, seasonal vegetables burst with color and flavor, embodying the rich bounty of the earth. A light and refreshing vinaigrette, infused with the essence of Water, brings all the elements together in perfect harmony. This is a customizable recipe, allowing you to celebrate the ever-changing offerings of summer's harvest.

Ingredients (Base recipe):

● **Salad:**

○ 4 cups mixed greens (such as baby spinach, arugula, or a combination)

○ 1 cup seasonal vegetables, chopped (such as cherry tomatoes, cucumber, bell peppers, corn kernels, or zucchini)

○ ½ cup crumbled feta cheese (optional)

- ○ ¼ cup pitted kalamata olives, halved (optional)

- ○ Fresh herbs, such as chopped basil, oregano, or parsley (optional)

- **Light Vinaigrette:**

  - ○ ¼ cup olive oil
  - ○ 2 tablespoons lemon juice
  - ○ 1 tablespoon balsamic vinegar (optional)
  - ○ 1 teaspoon Dijon mustard
  - ○ 1 teaspoon honey
  - ○ Salt and freshly ground black pepper, to taste

Conversions:
- 1 cup = 240 ml (US customary) or 250 ml (metric)
- 1 tablespoon = 15 ml
- 1 teaspoon = 5 ml

Tips:
- Use a variety of colorful and seasonal vegetables for a visually stunning and flavorful salad.
- Wash and dry your greens thoroughly to prevent a watery salad.
- Chop the vegetables into bite-sized pieces for even distribution of flavor and texture.
- The feta cheese and olives add a salty and briny element to the salad, but they can be omitted for a vegan option.
- Fresh herbs elevate the flavor of the salad. Choose your favorites based on the vegetables you use and your taste preference.

Allergy/Diet Differences:
- **Vegetarian:** This recipe is naturally vegetarian.
- **Vegan:** Omit the feta cheese and use a plant-based olive oil alternative for the vinaigrette.
- **Gluten-free:** This recipe is naturally gluten-free.

Instructions:

Vinaigrette:

1. In a small bowl, whisk together the olive oil, lemon juice, balsamic vinegar (if using), Dijon mustard, honey, salt, and pepper. Taste and adjust seasonings as desired.

Salad:

1. In a large bowl, combine the mixed greens and chopped vegetables.
2. Crumble the feta cheese (if using) and add it to the salad bowl along with the olives (if using) and fresh herbs (if using).
3. Pour the desired amount of vinaigrette over the salad and toss gently to coat.
4. Serve immediately and enjoy!

Variations:
- **Protein Power:** Add cooked grilled chicken, shrimp, or tofu to the salad for a more protein-rich option.
- **Fruity Twist:** Incorporate seasonal fruits like strawberries, blueberries, or peaches for a touch of sweetness.
- **Nutty Crunch:** Sprinkle toasted nuts like almonds, walnuts, or pecans over the salad for added texture and flavor.

● **Hearty Grains:** For a more substantial salad, add cooked quinoa, brown rice, or farro.

Embrace the vibrant energy of summer with this refreshing and customizable salad! Let the symphony of Earth and Water guide you as you explore the endless possibilities of seasonal ingredients.

Fruit Crumble: A Cozy Fusion of Earth and Fire

THIS COMFORTING FRUIT crumble embodies the essence of Earth and Fire. A base of rustic oat crumble, studded with earthy nuts and seeds, rests upon a bed of juicy, seasonal fruit. The warmth of the oven (Fire) transforms the crumble topping into a golden, crispy blanket, while the fruit softens and releases its vibrant flavors (Earth). This recipe offers a versatile base, allowing you to explore the abundance of nature's harvest throughout the year.

Ingredients (Base recipe):

● **Fruit Filling:**

○ 4-5 cups chopped seasonal fruit (such as apples, pears, berries, peaches, plums, or rhubarb)

- ○ ¼ cup granulated sugar (adjust based on the sweetness of your fruit)

- ○ 2 tablespoons cornstarch

- ○ 1 tablespoon lemon juice (optional, for fruits that tend to brown)

- **Crumble Topping:**

  - ○ 1 cup rolled oats
  - ○ ½ cup all-purpose flour
  - ○ ½ cup chopped nuts (such as almonds, pecans, or walnuts)
  - ○ ¼ cup packed light brown sugar
  - ○ ¼ cup unsalted butter, cold and cubed
  - ○ Pinch of salt
  - ○ Pinch of ground cinnamon

Conversions:
- 1 cup = 240 ml (US customary) or 250 ml (metric)
- 1 tablespoon = 15 ml
- ¼ cup = 60 ml

Tips:
- Choose fruits that are ripe but still hold their shape. Softer fruits will create a mushier filling.
- If using fruits that tend to brown quickly, such as apples, toss them with lemon juice to prevent discoloration.
- Adjust the amount of sugar based on the sweetness of your chosen fruit. Tart fruits may require more sugar, while very ripe fruits may need less.
- The cornstarch helps thicken the fruit filling slightly.
- Use a variety of chopped nuts for added texture and flavor. You can also substitute other chopped seeds, such as sunflower seeds or pumpkin seeds.
- Cold butter is key to achieving a crumbly topping. Cutting the cold butter into the dry ingredients creates small pockets of fat that melt during baking, resulting in a crispy texture.
- Feel free to adjust the spices in the crumble topping to complement your chosen fruit. A pinch of nutmeg or ginger can also be delightful additions.

Allergy/Diet Differences:
- **Vegetarian:** This recipe is naturally vegetarian.
- **Vegan:** This recipe can be adapted to be vegan. Use a vegan butter substitute and a gluten-free flour blend if needed.
- **Gluten-free:** Substitute the all-purpose flour with a 1:1 gluten-free baking flour blend.

Instructions:
Fruit Filling:

1. Preheat oven to 375°F (190°C).
2. In a large bowl, combine the chopped fruit, sugar, cornstarch, and lemon juice (if using). Toss to coat the fruit evenly.

Crumble Topping:

1. In a medium bowl, whisk together the rolled oats, flour, chopped nuts, brown sugar, salt, and cinnamon.
2. Using a pastry cutter or your fingertips, cut the cold cubed butter into the dry ingredients until the mixture resembles coarse crumbs.

Assembly and Baking:

1. Transfer the fruit filling to a baking dish (approximately 8x8 inch or 9x13 inch).
2. Sprinkle the crumble topping evenly over the fruit filling.
3. Bake for 40-50 minutes, or until the crumble topping is golden brown and the fruit filling is bubbling.

Tips:
- For a decorative touch, sprinkle the crumble topping with a tablespoon of rolled oats before baking.
- Serve the crumble warm or at room temperature, topped with a scoop of vanilla ice cream, whipped cream, or yogurt for an extra treat.

Embrace the comforting warmth of this dessert as Earth and Fire come together in perfect harmony. Explore the endless possibilities offered by seasonal fruits and create your own signature crumble!

Heavenly Meringue Cookies: A Dance of Air and Fire

THESE ETHEREAL MERINGUE cookies embody the essence of Air in their purest form. Light, airy, and impossibly delicate, they melt in your mouth with a whisper of sweetness. The touch of Fire from the oven transforms the egg whites into a billowy cloud, creating a delightful treat that celebrates Air's weightless spirit.

Ingredients:

- 3 large egg whites, at room temperature
- Pinch of cream of tartar
- ¾ cup (150g) granulated sugar
- ½ teaspoon vanilla extract (optional)

Conversions:

- 1 cup = 240 ml (US customary) or 250 ml (metric)
- 1 teaspoon = 5 ml

Tips:

- Use a clean, grease-free bowl for whipping the egg whites. Any trace of fat or yolk can prevent them from reaching stiff peaks.
- Allow the egg whites to come to room temperature for optimal volume when whisking. Cold egg whites take longer to whip and may not achieve the desired stiff peaks.
- The cream of tartar helps stabilize the egg whites and achieve stiffer peaks.
- Gradually add the sugar to the egg whites while whisking continuously. This ensures the sugar dissolves properly and creates a stable meringue.
- Don't overmix the meringue once you reach stiff peaks. Overmixing can deflate the air incorporated into the egg whites.
- Use a piping bag fitted with a star tip for easy and decorative shaping of the cookies. Alternatively, you can spoon dollops of meringue onto the baking sheet.
- Tap the baking sheet gently a few times on the counter to release any air bubbles trapped in the meringue.

Allergy/Diet Differences:
- **Vegetarian:** This recipe is naturally vegetarian.
- **Vegan:** Not vegan due to the reliance on egg whites.
- **Gluten-free:** This recipe is naturally gluten-free.

Instructions:

1. Preheat oven to 200°F (95°C). Line a baking sheet with parchment paper.
2. In a clean, grease-free bowl, whisk together the egg whites and cream of tartar on medium speed until soft peaks form.
3. Gradually increase the speed to high and continue whisking while slowly adding the sugar, one tablespoon at a time. Continue whisking until stiff peaks form. The peaks should be firm and hold their shape when the whisk is lifted.
4. If using, gently fold in the vanilla extract with a rubber spatula.
5. Spoon the meringue mixture into a piping bag fitted with a star tip, or simply spoon dollops of meringue onto the prepared baking sheet, leaving space between each cookie for spreading.
6. Bake for 1-1 ½ hours, or until the meringue cookies are dry and crisp to the touch. The cookies may develop a light golden color on the outside.
7. Turn off the oven and leave the cookies inside to cool completely for at least 1 hour. This slow drying process helps prevent cracks in the meringue.

These heavenly meringue cookies are a testament to the lightness and sweetness of Air. Enjoy them on their own or use them to create beautiful and delicious dessert decorations!

Airy Buttermilk Biscuits: A Celebration of Air and Water

THESE DELIGHTFUL BUTTERMILK biscuits embody the harmonious dance of Air and Water. Light and airy pockets grace the interior, thanks to the leavening power of baking powder and the gentle incorporation of buttermilk. Water weaves its magic by creating a moist and tender crumb. This recipe offers a classic base, with tips for achieving the airiest possible texture.

Ingredients:
● **Dry Ingredients:**

○ 2 ½ cups (310g) all-purpose flour
○ 2 tablespoons (25g) granulated sugar
○ 1 teaspoon (5g) baking powder
○ ½ teaspoon (2.5g) salt

● **Wet Ingredients:**

○ 1 cup (240ml) cold buttermilk
○ ½ cup (1 stick) unsalted butter, very cold and cubed
○ 1 tablespoon (15ml) melted butter (optional, for brushing tops)

Conversions:

● 1 cup = 240 ml (US customary) or 250 ml (metric)
● 1 tablespoon = 15 ml
● 1 teaspoon = 5 ml

Tips for Airy Perfection:

● **Cold is Key:** Use cold buttermilk and very cold butter. The cold butter creates pockets of fat that steam during baking, resulting in those beautiful air pockets.

● **Don't Overwork the Dough:** Once the dry and wet ingredients are combined, handle the dough as little as possible. Overworking will develop the gluten, leading to a denser biscuit.

● **Gently Fold:** Use a folding motion to incorporate the wet ingredients into the dry ingredients. This helps maintain air pockets within the dough.

● **Pat, Don't Knead:** Gently pat the dough into a square on a lightly floured surface. Avoid kneading or rolling, which can toughen the biscuits.

● **Cut Straight Down:** Use a sharp knife to cut the dough into squares. A sawing motion can compress the layers and prevent air from rising.

Allergy/Diet Differences:

● **Vegetarian:** This recipe is naturally vegetarian.

● **Vegan:** This recipe can be adapted to be vegan. Use a vegan buttermilk substitute (made with plant-based milk and vinegar or lemon juice) and a vegan butter alternative.

● **Gluten-free:** Not recommended for a gluten-free adaptation due to the reliance on wheat flour for structure.

Instructions:

1. Preheat oven to 450°F (230°C). Line a baking sheet with parchment paper.
2. In a large bowl, whisk together the flour, sugar, baking powder, and salt.
3. Cut the cold butter into cubes using a pastry cutter or two knives. Work quickly to keep the butter cold. You want a mixture of pea-sized and flour-coated butter pieces.
4. Add the cubed butter to the dry ingredients and toss to coat.
5. Make a well in the center of the dry ingredients. Pour in the cold buttermilk and gently fold it in with a rubber spatula until just combined. A few streaks of flour are okay.
6. Turn the dough out onto a lightly floured surface. Gently pat the dough into a square about 1 inch thick.
7. Using a sharp knife, cut the dough into 8-12 squares, depending on your desired biscuit size.
8. Place the biscuits on the prepared baking sheet, leaving space between them for spreading. Brush the tops with melted butter (optional).
9. Bake for 12-15 minutes, or until golden brown and risen.
10. Serve immediately while warm and enjoy the delightful dance of Air and Water in every bite!

Part 3: Fire (10 Recipes)

Embrace the Flame: Ignite Your Culinary Creativity

Fire, the transformative element, takes center stage in this section. Its essence is about passion, intensity, and the powerful ability to change and refine. As you explore the following recipes, discover how Fire translates into the culinary world through various techniques and ingredients.

Essence of Fire:

Fire's presence in the kitchen extends beyond the literal flames of your stovetop or oven. It encompasses the transformation of raw ingredients into delectable dishes, the sizzle of a perfectly seared steak, and the vibrant warmth of spices that tantalize the taste buds. Here's how Fire manifests in our culinary creations:

● **Transformative Techniques:** Grilling, searing, roasting, and smoking are all methods that utilize Fire's direct heat to create unique flavors and textures.

● **Kiss of the Flame:** Searing meat quickly at high temperatures creates a beautiful caramelized crust, locking in juices and adding depth of flavor.

● **Slow and Smoky:** Smoking imbues food with a subtle smokiness, infusing it with a complex and alluring aroma.

● **Spice Up Your Life:** Chili peppers, ginger, and other bold spices embody Fire's essence by adding heat and vibrancy to dishes.

The following 10 recipes will guide you on a fiery culinary adventure. Prepare to unlock the transformative power of Fire in your kitchen!

As you embark on this fiery journey, remember: Fire is a powerful tool. Use it with respect, and it will reward you with dishes that are not only delicious but also bursting with flavor and personality.

Seared Steaks with Fiery Chimichurri: A Dance of Fire and Earth

THIS RECIPE IGNITES the essence of Fire with perfectly seared steaks, while celebrating Earth's bounty with a vibrant chimichurri sauce. The high heat of the grill caramelizes the exterior of the steaks, locking in juicy tenderness. The chimichurri, a vibrant condiment bursting with fresh herbs and garlic, adds a touch of Earth's verdant soul.

Ingredients:

● **For the Steaks:**

○ 2 ribeye steaks (each about 1 inch thick) or your favorite cut

○ 1 tablespoon olive oil

○ Salt and freshly ground black pepper, to taste

● **For the Chimichurri Sauce:**

○ ½ cup (packed) fresh flat-leaf parsley leaves

- ○ ¼ cup fresh cilantro leaves
- ○ 2 garlic cloves, minced
- ○ 1 shallot, finely minced (optional)
- ○ 1/4 cup olive oil
- ○ 2 tablespoons red wine vinegar
- ○ 1 teaspoon fresh oregano leaves, chopped (or ½ teaspoon dried)
- ○ ½ teaspoon red pepper flakes (adjust to preference)
- ○ Salt and freshly ground black pepper, to taste

Conversions:
- 1 cup = 240 ml (US customary) or 250 ml (metric)
- 1 tablespoon = 15 ml
- ¼ cup = 60 ml

Tips:
- Choose steaks that are at least 1 inch thick for even cooking on the grill.
- Allow the steaks to come to room temperature for about 30 minutes before grilling. This ensures even cooking throughout.
- Pat the steaks dry with paper towels before seasoning. Excess moisture can prevent a good sear.
- Use a cast-iron grill pan or preheat your outdoor grill to high heat for optimal searing.
- Don't overcook the steaks! Aim for an internal temperature of 125°F (52°C) for rare, 135°F (57°C) for medium-rare, or 145°F (63°C) for medium-done.
- Let the cooked steaks rest for a few minutes before slicing. This allows the juices to redistribute for a more flavorful and tender bite.

Allergy/Diet Differences:
- **Vegetarian:** Substitute portobello mushroom steaks for the beef steaks. Marinate the mushrooms in a mixture of olive oil, balsamic vinegar, soy sauce, and spices for a flavorful vegetarian option.
- **Vegan:** This recipe is not vegan due to the use of steaks. Consider the vegetarian portobello mushroom option for a vegan adaptation.
- **Gluten-free:** This recipe is naturally gluten-free.

Instructions:

Chimichurri Sauce:

1. In a food processor or blender, combine the parsley, cilantro, garlic, shallot (if using), olive oil, red wine vinegar, oregano, red pepper flakes, salt, and pepper. Pulse until a chunky sauce forms. You can also finely chop the herbs by hand for a more rustic texture.
2. Set the chimichurri sauce aside to allow the flavors to meld.

Grilled Steaks:

1. Brush the steaks with olive oil and season generously with salt and pepper.
2. Preheat your grill or cast-iron grill pan to high heat.
3. Sear the steaks for 2-3 minutes per side for a rare to medium-rare doneness.
4. Remove the steaks from the grill and let them rest on a cutting board for 5-10 minutes before slicing.

Serve the seared steaks with a generous spooning of chimichurri sauce. Enjoy the fiery dance between the heat of the grilled steaks and the verdant flavors of the chimichurri!

Fiery Stir-Fry Symphony: Earth and Fire in Harmony (Variation: Embrace the Water Element)

THIS RECIPE IGNITES a vibrant symphony of Earth and Fire. Savory ground meat and crisp vegetables, representing Earth's bounty, are stir-fried with a fiery sauce that awakens the essence of Fire. The classic recipe offers a bold and flavorful experience, while the variation introduces a touch of Water with a light broth, creating a more balanced and soothing taste profile.

Ingredients (Classic Recipe):

● **Stir-Fry Base:**

○ 1 tablespoon vegetable oil

○ 1 pound (450g) ground chicken or turkey

○ 1 medium onion, chopped

○ 1 red bell pepper, chopped

○ 2 cloves garlic, minced

○ 1 inch ginger, grated

● **Spicy Stir-Fry Sauce:**

○ ¼ cup soy sauce

○ 2 tablespoons brown sugar

○ 1 tablespoon rice vinegar

○ 1 tablespoon sriracha sauce (adjust to preference)

○ 1 teaspoon cornstarch

○ ½ teaspoon sesame oil

● **Noodles:**

○ 8 ounces (225g) dried noodles (such as rice noodles, lo mein, or ramen)

○ Cooked and chopped vegetables of your choice (such as broccoli florets, carrots, snow peas)

● **Garnishes (optional):**

○ Chopped green onions

○ Toasted sesame seeds

Conversions:

● 1 cup = 240 ml (US customary) or 250 ml (metric)

● 1 tablespoon = 15 ml

● 1 pound = 450g

● 1 inch = 2.54cm

Tips:

● Lean ground meat (around 90% lean) works best for this recipe.

● Feel free to substitute other protein options like tofu or tempeh for a vegetarian variation.

● Prepare all your ingredients beforehand for a smooth stir-frying experience.

● Use high heat and cook the ingredients in batches to avoid overcrowding the pan, which can steam the vegetables instead of searing them.

● The cornstarch in the sauce helps thicken it slightly. Mix it with a splash of water or broth to create a slurry before adding it to the pan.

Allergy/Diet Differences:

● **Vegetarian:** Substitute ground tofu or tempeh for the chicken or turkey.

● **Vegan:** Use a plant-based ground meat alternative and a vegan soy sauce substitute for the sauce.

● **Gluten-free:** Choose gluten-free noodles like rice noodles or bean thread noodles.

Instructions (Classic Recipe):

1. Cook the noodles according to package instructions. Drain and set aside.

2. Heat the vegetable oil in a large wok or skillet over high heat. Add the ground meat and cook until browned, breaking it up with a spoon as it cooks.
3. Add the onion, bell pepper, garlic, and ginger to the pan and stir-fry for 3-4 minutes, or until softened.
4. In a small bowl, whisk together the soy sauce, brown sugar, rice vinegar, sriracha sauce, cornstarch, and sesame oil.
5. Pour the sauce into the pan with the stir-fry mixture and bring to a simmer. Cook until the sauce thickens slightly.
6. Add the cooked noodles and any additional vegetables of your choice to the pan and toss to coat them in the sauce.
7. Serve immediately, garnished with chopped green onions and toasted sesame seeds (optional).

Variation: Embrace the Water Element with a Light Broth
For a more balanced and slightly lighter stir-fry, incorporate a touch of Water by adding a light broth to the sauce.
● **Additional Ingredient:**

   ○ ½ cup (120ml) chicken or vegetable broth

Variation Instructions:

1. Follow steps 1-4 of the Classic Recipe instructions.
2. In a small bowl, whisk together the soy sauce, brown sugar, rice vinegar, sriracha sauce, cornstarch, sesame oil, and **chicken or vegetable broth.**
3. Follow steps 5-7 of the Classic Recipe instructions.

This recipe is a testament to the harmonious interplay of Earth and Fire. Explore the classic recipe for a bold and fiery experience, or embrace the Water variation for a more balanced and comforting stir-fry. Enjoy!

Caribbean Jerk Chicken with Pineapple Salsa: A Symphony of Fire and Earth

THIS RECIPE TAKES YOU on a vibrant journey to the Caribbean, celebrating the fiery spirit of Fire and the rich bounty of Earth. Jerk seasoning, a fiery blend of spices, infuses the chicken with bold flavors, while the accompanying pineapple salsa adds a touch of sweet and tangy Earth to the dish.

Ingredients:

● **Jerk Chicken:**

○ 1 pound (450g) boneless, skinless chicken breasts or thighs

○ 2 tablespoons olive oil

○ 1 tablespoon brown sugar

○ 1 tablespoon soy sauce

○ 1 tablespoon lime juice

○ 1 scotch bonnet pepper, seeded and finely chopped (adjust to preference for spice level)

○ 1 habanero pepper, seeded and finely chopped (optional, for extra heat)

○ 1 teaspoon allspice berries, ground

○ 1 teaspoon dried thyme

○ ½ teaspoon ground nutmeg

○ ½ teaspoon ground ginger

○ ¼ teaspoon ground cinnamon

○ Salt and freshly ground black pepper, to taste

● **Pineapple Salsa:**

○ 1 cup (150g) fresh pineapple, diced
○ ½ red onion, finely diced
○ 1 jalapeno pepper, seeded and finely chopped (optional, for spice)
○ ¼ cup fresh cilantro, chopped
○ 1 tablespoon lime juice
○ 1 tablespoon olive oil
○ Salt and freshly ground black pepper, to taste

Conversions:
● 1 cup = 240 ml (US customary) or 250 ml (metric)
● 1 tablespoon = 15 ml
● 1 pound = 450g
Tips:
● Marinate the chicken for at least 30 minutes, or ideally overnight, for maximum flavor infusion.
● If using fresh scotch bonnet or habanero peppers, wear gloves while handling them to avoid burning your skin.
● The jerk seasoning can be quite spicy. Adjust the amount of scotch bonnet pepper or habanero pepper to your preference.
● Use a grill pan or outdoor grill for a smoky flavor, or bake the chicken in the oven for a more convenient option.
Allergy/Diet Differences:
● **Vegetarian:** Substitute tofu or tempeh steaks for the chicken and marinate them in the jerk seasoning for a flavorful vegetarian option.
● **Vegan:** Use a vegan marinade substitute and omit the honey in the salsa (if using). Opt for a plant-based olive oil alternative.
● **Gluten-free:** This recipe is naturally gluten-free.
Instructions:
Jerk Chicken:

1. In a small bowl, whisk together the olive oil, brown sugar, soy sauce, lime juice, scotch bonnet pepper, habanero pepper (if using), allspice berries, thyme, nutmeg, ginger, cinnamon, salt, and pepper.
2. Place the chicken in a shallow dish and pour the marinade over it. Coat the chicken evenly and marinate for at least 30 minutes, or preferably overnight, in the refrigerator.
3. Preheat your grill pan or outdoor grill to medium-high heat. Alternatively, preheat your oven to 400°F (200°C).
4. If grilling, cook the chicken for 5-7 minutes per side, or until cooked through. If baking, bake for 20-25 minutes, or until the internal temperature of the chicken reaches 165°F (74°C).
5. Let the chicken rest for 5-10 minutes before slicing.

Pineapple Salsa:

1. In a medium bowl, combine the diced pineapple, red onion, jalapeno pepper (if using), cilantro, lime juice, olive oil, salt, and pepper. Toss to coat evenly.

Serve the jerk chicken with the refreshing pineapple salsa. Enjoy the fiery dance of jerk seasoning with the sweet and tangy flavors of the pineapple salsa!

Seared Scallops with Creamy Risotto: A Celebration of Earth and Water

THIS RECIPE EMBODIES the harmonious dance between Earth and Water. Perfectly seared scallops, representing the essence of Earth's bounty, rest upon a bed of creamy risotto, a dish synonymous with Water's nurturing qualities. The classic recipe offers a luxurious and elegant main course, while the variation incorporates a touch of earthy luxury with truffle oil.

Ingredients (Classic Recipe):

● **For the Scallops:**

○ 1 pound (450g) large sea scallops
○ 2 tablespoons olive oil
○ Salt and freshly ground black pepper, to taste

● **For the Creamy Risotto:**

○ 4 cups (1L) low-sodium chicken or vegetable broth, heated and kept simmering

○ 2 tablespoons olive oil

○ 1 shallot, finely chopped

○ 1 cup (200g) Arborio rice

○ ½ cup (120ml) dry white wine

○ ½ cup grated Parmesan cheese

○ 2 tablespoons unsalted butter

○ Chopped fresh parsley, for garnish (optional)

Conversions:
- 1 cup = 240 ml (US customary) or 250 ml (metric)
- 1 tablespoon = 15 ml
- 1 pound = 450g

Tips:
- Purchase dry sea scallops for the best searing results. Wet or previously frozen scallops can release excess moisture, hindering a good sear.
- Pat the scallops dry very thoroughly with paper towels before searing. Excess moisture will prevent a beautiful golden brown crust.
- Use a heavy-bottomed pan or skillet for even heat distribution when searing the scallops.
- Don't overcook the scallops! They should be opaque throughout with a slightly translucent center for optimal texture.

Allergy/Diet Differences:
- **Vegetarian:** Omit the scallops and focus on a flavorful vegetable risotto. Consider using roasted vegetables like butternut squash or asparagus for added earthiness. Substitute vegetable broth for the chicken broth.
- **Vegan:** This recipe is not vegan due to the scallops and Parmesan cheese. Opt for a vegan risotto recipe and substitute the scallops with pan-fried tofu or portobello mushrooms.
- **Gluten-free:** Substitute Arborio rice with gluten-free brown rice or another recommended gluten-free risotto rice variety.

Instructions (Classic Recipe):
Creamy Risotto:

1. Heat the chicken or vegetable broth in a saucepan or pot and bring it to a simmer. Keep it simmering throughout the risotto cooking process.
2. In a separate large pan or Dutch oven, heat the olive oil over medium heat. Add the shallot and cook until softened, about 2-3 minutes.
3. Add the Arborio rice and stir to coat it with the oil. Cook for about 1 minute, stirring constantly, until the rice becomes translucent.
4. Pour in the white wine and cook, stirring constantly, until the wine is absorbed by the rice.
5. Start adding the hot broth, ½ cup at a time, stirring constantly after each addition. Allow the rice to absorb

the broth before adding the next ladleful. This process takes about 18-20 minutes, or until the rice is cooked through but still has a slight bite (al dente).

6. Once the rice is cooked, remove the pan from the heat and stir in the Parmesan cheese and butter. Season with salt and pepper to taste.

Seared Scallops:

1. Pat the scallops dry very thoroughly with paper towels. Season them generously with salt and pepper.
2. Heat a heavy-bottomed pan or skillet over medium-high heat. Add the olive oil and swirl to coat the pan.
3. When the oil is hot and shimmering, carefully add the scallops. Sear the scallops for 2-3 minutes per side, undisturbed, or until golden brown and opaque throughout with a slightly translucent center.

To Serve:

1. Spoon the creamy risotto onto plates. Top each serving with the seared scallops.
2. Garnish with chopped fresh parsley (optional) and serve immediately.

Variation: Incorporate Earthy Elements with Truffle Oil

For an extra touch of luxury and earthiness, add a few drops of truffle oil to the finished risotto just before serving. Swirl it gently to distribute the truffle oil's aroma and flavor throughout the dish.

Enjoy the harmonious interplay of Earth and Water in this elegant dish. The classic recipe offers a timeless combination, while the truffle oil variation adds a touch of decadence. Savor the delicate flavors of the seared scallops and the comforting embrace of the creamy risotto!

Roasted Cauliflower with Smoky Embrace: A Celebration of Earth and Fire

THIS RECIPE CELEBRATES the harmonious union of Earth and Fire. Earthy cauliflower florets are transformed by Fire's gentle kiss, taking on a smoky depth of flavor thanks to paprika. Simple and versatile, this dish can be enjoyed as a flavorful side or incorporated into other creations.

Ingredients:

- 1 head of cauliflower, about 1-1.5 pounds (450-680g)
- 2 tablespoons olive oil
- 1 tablespoon smoked paprika
- 1/2 teaspoon garlic powder
- 1/4 teaspoon onion powder
- Salt and freshly ground black pepper, to taste
- Fresh herbs (optional, for garnish): Chopped parsley, chives, or thyme

Conversions:

- 1 pound = 450g

Tips:

- Choose a head of cauliflower with firm, white florets for the best results.
- Cutting the cauliflower into similar-sized florets ensures even cooking.
- Don't overcrowd the baking sheet. This allows for better air circulation and even browning.
- Roasting vegetables at a high temperature helps achieve tender florets with a slightly caramelized exterior.

Allergy/Diet Differences:

- **Vegetarian:** This recipe is naturally vegetarian.
- **Vegan:** This recipe is naturally vegan.
- **Gluten-free:** This recipe is naturally gluten-free.

Instructions:

1. Preheat your oven to 425°F (220°C). Line a baking sheet with parchment paper.
2. Wash and dry the cauliflower head. Cut off the core and leaves, then break or cut the cauliflower into bite-sized florets.
3. In a large bowl, toss the cauliflower florets with olive oil, smoked paprika, garlic powder, onion powder, salt, and pepper. Ensure all the florets are evenly coated.
4. Spread the seasoned cauliflower florets in a single layer on the prepared baking sheet.
5. Roast the cauliflower for 20-25 minutes, or until the florets are tender and slightly browned on the edges. You can test for doneness by piercing a floret with a fork - it should slide in easily.
6. Remove the roasted cauliflower from the oven and let it cool slightly before serving.

Serving Suggestions:

- Enjoy the roasted cauliflower on its own as a flavorful side dish.
- Drizzle with a squeeze of lemon juice or a sprinkle of balsamic vinegar for a touch of acidity.
- Top with toasted nuts and a sprinkle of nutritional yeast for added flavor and texture.
- Use the roasted cauliflower florets in Buddha bowls, salads, or grain bowls for a nutritious and flavorful addition. Garnish with fresh chopped herbs like parsley, chives, or thyme (optional) for an extra touch of color and freshness.

This simple recipe allows the essence of Earth and Fire to shine through. Enjoy the smoky depth infused by the paprika and the tender texture of the roasted cauliflower. Let this dish be a versatile addition to your culinary repertoire!

Blackened Fish Tacos: A Dance of Fire and Earth (Variation: Embrace the Water Element)

THIS RECIPE IGNITES a fiery fiesta on your taste buds, celebrating the dynamic duo of Earth and Fire. Blackened fish, seasoned with a bold spice blend, embodies Fire's transformative touch. Earthy corn tortillas cradle the fish, while fresh toppings complete this flavorful symphony. The classic recipe offers a vibrant and spicy experience, while the variation incorporates a cooling slaw, introducing a touch of Water for a more balanced and refreshing taste.

Ingredients (Classic Recipe):

● **Blackened Fish:**

○ 1 pound (450g) firm white fish fillets (such as mahi-mahi, cod, or tilapia)

○ 2 tablespoons olive oil

○ 1 tablespoon smoked paprika

○ 1 teaspoon chili powder

○ 1 teaspoon cumin

○ ½ teaspoon garlic powder

○ ½ teaspoon onion powder

○ ¼ teaspoon cayenne pepper (adjust to preference)

○ Salt and freshly ground black pepper, to taste

● **Taco Accoutrements:**

○ 6-8 corn tortillas, warmed

○ Chopped fresh cilantro

○ Lime wedges

○ Optional toppings (choose your favorites): diced avocado, crumbled queso fresco, pico de gallo

Conversions:
● 1 pound = 450g
● 1 tablespoon = 15 ml

Tips:
● Choose firm white fish fillets that can withstand the heat of searing.
● Pat the fish dry thoroughly before seasoning to ensure the spices adhere well.
● Use a cast-iron skillet or grill pan for optimal heat distribution and a nice sear.
● Don't overcook the fish! Aim for an opaque interior with a slight flakiness for the best texture.

Allergy/Diet Differences:
● **Vegetarian:** Substitute portobello mushroom caps for the fish fillets. Marinate the mushrooms in a mixture of olive oil, soy sauce, lime juice, and spices for a flavorful vegetarian option.
● **Vegan:** Use a plant-based fish alternative and a vegan mayo or crema for the slaw (if using the variation). Opt for a plant-based olive oil alternative.
● **Gluten-free:** Choose corn tortillas certified gluten-free.

Instructions (Classic Recipe):
Blackened Fish:

1. In a small bowl, combine the olive oil, smoked paprika, chili powder, cumin, garlic powder, onion powder, cayenne pepper, salt, and pepper.
2. Pat the fish fillets dry with paper towels. Season them generously on both sides with the prepared spice mixture.
3. Heat a cast-iron skillet or grill pan over medium-high heat. Add a thin layer of oil.
4. When the pan is hot and shimmering, carefully add the fish fillets. Sear for 2-3 minutes per side, or until cooked through and slightly flaky.

Assemble the Tacos:

1. Warm the corn tortillas according to package instructions.
2. Place a cooked fish fillet on each warmed tortilla.
3. Add your desired toppings, such as chopped fresh cilantro, lime wedges, avocado, queso fresco, or pico de gallo.
4. Serve immediately and enjoy the fiery flavors!

Variation: Embrace the Water Element with a Cooling Slaw

For a more balanced and refreshing take on these tacos, incorporate a cooling slaw using the Water element. Here's what you'll need:

- **Cooling Slaw:**

  - 2 cups (200g) shredded cabbage (green or red)
  - ½ cup (125g) shredded carrots
  - ¼ cup (60ml) mayonnaise or vegan mayo (for vegan option)
  - 1 tablespoon lime juice
  - 1 tablespoon chopped fresh cilantro
  - Salt and freshly ground black pepper, to taste

Variation Instructions:

1. Follow steps 1-4 of the Classic Recipe instructions for blackening the fish.
2. While the fish cooks, prepare the cooling slaw. In a medium bowl, combine the shredded cabbage, carrots, mayonnaise or vegan mayo, lime juice, cilantro, salt, and pepper. Toss to coat evenly.
3. Assemble the tacos as instructed in the Classic Recipe, adding a spoonful of the cooling slaw alongside your other desired toppings.

This recipe is a testament to the harmonious interplay of Fire and Earth. Savor the bold flavors of the blackened fish and the comforting embrace of the corn tortillas. Explore the classic recipe for a fiery experience, or embrace the Water variation for a refreshing and balanced taco fiesta!

The Cauldron's Bounty: A Spicy Chili Symphony (Embracing All the Elements)

THIS RECIPE INVITES you to stir up a pot of magic in your very own kitchen. A hearty chili, representing the rich abundance of Earth, is infused with Fire's warmth and spice. This recipe is a base for exploration, encouraging the incorporation of all the elements – Air, Water, and Spirit – through a variety of toppings and accompaniments.

Ingredients (Basic Chili):

● **Earth's Bounty:**

○ 1 tablespoon olive oil

○ 1 pound (450g) ground beef or turkey (optional, omit for vegetarian chili)

○ 1 medium onion, chopped

○ 2 cloves garlic, minced

○ 1 green bell pepper, chopped (optional, for a touch of Air)

○ 1 red bell pepper, chopped (optional, for a touch of Fire)

○ 1 (15 oz) can diced tomatoes, undrained

○ 1 (15 oz) can kidney beans, drained and rinsed

○ 1 (15 oz) can black beans, drained and rinsed

○ 1 (15 oz) can pinto beans, drained and rinsed (optional, for extra Earthly abundance)

○ 4 cups (1L) low-sodium beef broth or vegetable broth (Water)

- **Fire's Kiss:**

○ 2 tablespoons chili powder
○ 1 teaspoon ground cumin
○ 1/2 teaspoon smoked paprika
○ 1/4 teaspoon cayenne pepper (adjust to preference)
○ Salt and freshly ground black pepper, to taste

Conversions:
- 1 cup = 240 ml (US customary) or 250 ml (metric)
- 1 tablespoon = 15 ml
- 1 pound = 450g

Tips:
- Browning the meat before adding other ingredients adds depth of flavor.
- Diced tomatoes with their juices provide a base for the chili's liquid.
- Rinsing the beans helps remove excess sodium and improve their texture.
- Adjust the level of spice according to your preference. Start with less cayenne pepper and add more to taste.

Allergy/Diet Differences:
- **Vegetarian:** Omit the ground meat and use vegetable broth instead of beef broth.
- **Vegan:** Use vegetable broth and omit cheese and sour cream from the toppings. Choose vegan chili beans and ensure all other ingredients are vegan-friendly.
- **Gluten-free:** Ensure all chosen toppings are gluten-free. Most chili ingredients are naturally gluten-free, but double-check labels.

Embracing All the Elements:

This recipe acts as a base, and you are invited to incorporate the other elements through your toppings and accompaniments. Here are some ideas:
- **Air:** Chopped fresh herbs like cilantro or chives add a touch of Air's lightness.
- **Water:** A dollop of sour cream or plain yogurt provides a cooling and creamy counterpoint to the spice.
- **Spirit:** A drizzle of your favorite hot sauce infuses the chili with your personal touch and a fiery spirit.

Classic Toppings Bar:
- Shredded cheddar cheese
- Diced red onion

- Chopped fresh cilantro or chives
- Sliced jalapenos (for the more adventurous)
- Sour cream or plain yogurt
- Hot sauce
- Lime wedges

Instructions:

1. In a large pot or Dutch oven, heat olive oil over medium heat. Add the ground meat (if using) and cook until browned, breaking it up with a spoon as it cooks. Drain any excess fat.
2. Add the onion, bell peppers (if using), and garlic to the pot and cook until softened, about 5 minutes.
3. Stir in the diced tomatoes, kidney beans, black beans, pinto beans (if using), chili powder, cumin, smoked paprika, cayenne pepper, salt, and pepper.
4. Pour in the broth and bring to a boil. Reduce heat to low, cover, and simmer for 30 minutes, or until the chili has thickened and the flavors have melded. Taste and adjust seasonings as needed.
5. While the chili simmers, prepare your desired toppings.

Serving Suggestions:
- Ladle the chili into bowls and serve hot with your chosen toppings.
- Accompany the chili with crusty bread for dipping or a side salad for a well-rounded meal.

The Final Touches

This recipe offers a framework for a delicious and customizable chili. Feel free to experiment with different vegetables, spices, and beans to create your own unique version. Here are some additional thoughts and ideas:

- **Leftovers:** Chili is a great dish for leftovers. It often tastes even better the next day as the flavors continue to develop. Store leftovers in an airtight container in the refrigerator for up to 3 days or freeze for longer storage.

- **Slow Cooker Option:** This chili can be easily adapted for a slow cooker. Simply brown the meat (if using) in a pan as directed, then add all ingredients to the slow cooker. Cook on low for 6-8 hours or on high for 3-4 hours.

- **Spicy vs. Mild:** This recipe offers a base level of spice. If you prefer a milder chili, reduce the amount of cayenne pepper or omit it altogether. For an extra kick, add chopped jalapenos or a sprinkle of red pepper flakes during cooking.

With this recipe as your guide, you can create a pot of chili that is both comforting and exciting. Let the elements be your inspiration, and enjoy the delicious alchemy that takes place in your kitchen!

Alchemy on the Grill: A Symphony of Fire and Earth (Endless Variations for Grilled Pizzas)

THIS RECIPE INVITES you to become a pizzaiolo under the open sky. Fire's transformative kiss awakens the essence of Earth's bounty in the form of a perfectly grilled pizza crust. This versatile recipe provides a foundation for endless variations, allowing you to create pizzas that reflect your tastes and dietary needs.

Ingredients (Basic Pizza Dough):

● **Earth's Foundation:**

- ○ 1 cup (240ml) warm water (105°F/40°C)
- ○ 1 teaspoon active dry yeast
- ○ 1 tablespoon olive oil
- ○ 3 cups (375g) all-purpose flour, plus extra for dusting
- ○ 1 teaspoon salt

For the Grill:
- Pizza stone (optional, for even heat distribution)
- Semolina flour or cornmeal, for dusting

Tips:
- Use warm water to activate the yeast. Hot water will kill the yeast, and cold water will slow down its activation.
- Kneading the dough develops the gluten, resulting in a chewier crust.
- Allowing the dough to rise gives the yeast time to ferment and creates a lighter and airier crust.
- A preheated pizza stone on the grill helps achieve a crispy bottom crust.

Allergy/Diet Differences:
- **Vegetarian:** All pizza toppings can be vegetarian. Opt for cheese made with rennet substitutes for a vegetarian option.
- **Vegan:** Use a vegan pizza dough recipe and vegan cheese alternatives for the toppings.
- **Gluten-free:** Use a gluten-free pizza dough recipe or a pre-made gluten-free pizza crust.

Endless Variations:
This recipe offers a blank canvas for your pizza creations. Here are some topping inspirations categorized by element:
- **Earth:** Roasted vegetables (peppers, onions, mushrooms), caramelized onions, various cheeses, pesto sauce, fresh herbs.
- **Fire:** Spicy sausage, pepperoni, hot peppers (jalapenos, chili flakes), sriracha drizzle.
- **Water:** Fresh mozzarella, ricotta cheese, tomato sauce, marinated artichoke hearts.
- **Air:** Light and airy toppings like thinly sliced prosciutto, arugula salad (added after grilling), shaved fennel.

Instructions (Basic Pizza Dough):

1. In a large bowl, combine the warm water, yeast, and olive oil. Let it sit for 5 minutes, or until the yeast becomes foamy.
2. Add the flour and salt to the wet ingredients. Stir with a wooden spoon until a shaggy dough forms.
3. Turn the dough out onto a lightly floured surface and knead for 10 minutes, or until smooth and elastic. Add more flour as needed to prevent sticking.
4. Place the dough in a greased bowl, cover it with plastic wrap, and let it rise in a warm place for 1-2 hours, or until doubled in size.

Preparing for the Grill:

1. Preheat your grill to medium-high heat. If using a pizza stone, preheat it on the grill for at least 30 minutes.
2. Lightly dust a work surface with semolina flour or cornmeal. Roll out the dough to your desired thickness.

Assembling and Grilling:

1. Transfer the rolled-out dough to a pizza peel or a large baking sheet dusted with semolina flour or cornmeal.
2. Spread your desired sauce and toppings onto the dough, leaving a slight border around the edge.
3. Carefully slide the pizza onto the preheated pizza stone (if using) or directly onto the grill grates.
4. Grill the pizza for 3-5 minutes per side, or until the crust is golden brown and the cheese is melted and bubbly. Use a grill spatula to turn the pizza as needed to ensure even cooking.

Serving Suggestions:

1. Slice the pizza and serve immediately.

2. Drizzle with olive oil, balsamic glaze, or hot sauce for an extra touch of flavor (optional).
3. Enjoy your creation under the open sky!

With this recipe as your guide, you can become a master of the open flame. Experiment with different topping combinations, and let your creativity flow. Remember, pizza-making on the grill is an alchemy of Fire and Earth, with endless possibilities for delicious results!

Heavenly Bites on the Grill: A Symphony of Fire and Air (Grilled Fruit Skewers with Honey Glaze)

THIS RECIPE INVITES you to celebrate the harmonious dance between Fire and Air. Seasonal fruits, representing Air's lightness and vibrancy, are transformed by Fire's gentle kiss on the grill, taking on a smoky depth of flavor. A simple honey glaze adds a touch of Earth's sweetness, creating heavenly bites that are perfect for a light dessert or a refreshing summer treat.

Ingredients:
- **Air's Bounty (choose your favorites):**

  - 1 cup (150g) fresh pineapple, cut into chunks
  - ½ cup (75g) strawberries, hulled
  - ½ cup (75g) blueberries
  - ½ cup (75g) cantaloupe, cut into chunks
  - ½ cup (75g) peaches, cut into wedges
  - (Optional) Other seasonal fruits like mango, kiwi, or watermelon

- **For the Skewers:**

  - Wooden skewers, soaked in water for at least 30 minutes (to prevent burning)

- **Honey Glaze:**

  - ¼ cup (60ml) honey
  - 1 tablespoon (15ml) lemon juice
  - Pinch of ground cinnamon (optional)

Conversions:
- 1 cup = 240 ml (US customary) or 250 ml (metric)
- 1 tablespoon = 15 ml

Tips:
- Choose firm and ripe fruits that will hold their shape well on the grill.
- Soaking the skewers in water prevents them from burning during grilling.
- Cut the fruits into similar sizes for even cooking.
- Baste the fruit skewers with the honey glaze frequently for a caramelized and flavorful finish.

Allergy/Diet Differences:
- **Vegetarian:** This recipe is naturally vegetarian.
- **Vegan:** Use a vegan honey substitute for the glaze. Opt for fruits like pineapple, mango, and berries that don't require basting with honey.
- **Gluten-free:** This recipe is naturally gluten-free.

Instructions:

Honey Glaze:

1. In a small saucepan, combine the honey, lemon juice, and optional cinnamon. Heat over low heat until the honey dissolves and the mixture becomes slightly syrupy. Set aside.

Preparing the Fruit Skewers:

1. Assemble the skewers by threading your chosen fruits onto the soaked wooden skewers. Alternate colors and textures for a visually appealing presentation.

Grilling the Skewers:

1. Preheat your grill to medium-high heat.
2. Lightly oil the grill grates to prevent sticking.
3. Place the fruit skewers on the preheated grill.
4. Grill the skewers for 2-3 minutes per side, or until lightly charred and the fruits are warmed through.
5. Brush the fruit skewers generously with the honey glaze while grilling, turning them frequently to ensure even coating.

Serving Suggestions:

1. Transfer the grilled fruit skewers to a plate.
2. Drizzle with any remaining honey glaze.
3. Serve warm or at room temperature.
4. Enjoy these heavenly bites on their own or with a dollop of whipped cream or vanilla yogurt (optional).

With this recipe as your guide, you can celebrate the magic of Fire and Air. Experiment with different fruit combinations and let the flavors dance on your tongue. May these grilled fruit skewers become a delightful addition to your summer gatherings!

Molten Magic: A Fiery Symphony of Earth and Air (Flaming Chocolate Lava Cakes)

THIS RECIPE INVITES you to witness a captivating display of Fire and Air. Rich chocolate cakes, representing Earth's bounty, transform into molten pools of decadence with a touch of Fire. A dramatic tableside flourish, incorporating flaming spirits, adds an element of Air, creating a truly unforgettable dessert experience.

Ingredients:

● **Earth's Indulgence:**

○ 4 ounces (113g) dark chocolate, chopped (60-70% cacao content recommended)

○ 4 tablespoons (60ml) unsalted butter

○ 2 large eggs

○ 1/2 cup (100g) granulated sugar

○ 1/4 cup (30g) all-purpose flour

○ Pinch of salt

● **For the Flambe (Optional, with Safety Precautions):**

○ 2 tablespoons (30ml) high-proof rum or brandy (**Use with extreme caution! Flambe only under adult supervision and away from flammable objects**)

○ 1 tablespoon (15ml) granulated sugar

Conversions:
● 1 cup = 240 ml (US customary) or 250 ml (metric)
● 1 tablespoon = 15 ml
● 1 ounce = 28g

Tips:
● Use high-quality dark chocolate for the best flavor.
● Separate the eggs at room temperature for easier separation.
● Don't overmix the batter. A few lumps are okay.
● Baking time is crucial. Undercooked cakes will be runny, while overcooked cakes will lose their molten center.

Allergy/Diet Differences:
● **Vegetarian:** This recipe is naturally vegetarian.
● **Vegan:** Opt for a vegan chocolate and butter substitute. There are many vegan lava cake recipes available online.
● **Gluten-free:** Use a gluten-free flour blend in place of all-purpose flour. Ensure all other ingredients are certified gluten-free.

Safety Precautions for Flambe (if using):
● Flambe should only be done by adults and with extreme caution.
● Never leave a flaming pan unattended.
● Keep a fire extinguisher nearby in case of emergencies.
● Ensure the alcohol is heated until the fumes ignite, not the liquid itself.
● Do not flambé near flammable objects or flowing fabrics.

Instructions:
Chocolate Lava Cakes:

1. Preheat your oven to 425°F (220°C). Lightly grease four ramekins or small oven-safe baking dishes.
2. In a heat-resistant bowl set over a pot of simmering water (double boiler), melt the chopped chocolate and butter together until smooth. Stir occasionally. Remove from heat and let cool slightly.
3. In a separate bowl, whisk together the eggs and sugar until light and fluffy.
4. Sift the flour and salt into the chocolate mixture and fold it in gently with a spatula until just combined. Do not overmix.
5. Gently fold the egg mixture into the chocolate mixture until just incorporated.
6. Divide the batter evenly among the prepared ramekins.

Baking and Serving:

1. Bake the lava cakes for 8-10 minutes, or until the edges are set but the centers are still wobbly.
2. **Optional Flambe (Use with extreme caution):** While the cakes are still hot from the oven, carefully heat the rum or brandy in a small saucepan until warm. Do not let it boil. Light the alcohol vapors with a long match or lighter (away from the pan). Tilt the pan slightly and pour the flaming liquid over each lava cake. **Extinguish the flames immediately** by spooning the hot liquid back into the pan.
3. Serve the lava cakes immediately with a dusting of powdered sugar, a dollop of whipped cream, or vanilla ice cream (optional).

With this recipe, you've become an alchemist, transforming Earth's bounty into a decadent dessert. The rich chocolate and the dramatic presentation with the optional flambe create a symphony of flavors and textures. Remember, safety is paramount when using alcohol for flambe. Enjoy these molten marvels responsibly!

Part 4: Water - Embracing the Flow

Water, the essence of life, embodies adaptability, nurturance, and the constant flow that sustains us. In the kitchen, water plays a crucial role in various cooking methods, transforming ingredients and creating flavorful dishes. This section delves into the magic of Water, exploring ten recipes that showcase its versatility and the techniques that unlock its potential.

Essence of Water:

Water's adaptability allows it to exist in various states – solid (ice), liquid (water itself), and gas (steam). In cooking, we harness these different forms to achieve diverse results. Water can:

- **Dissolve:** It dissolves salt and other flavorings, creating flavorful broths and stocks.
- **Simmer:** Gentle heat and water create a nurturing environment for slow cooking, resulting in tender meats and vegetables.
- **Poach:** Submerging delicate ingredients in simmering water preserves their texture and allows flavors to infuse gently.
- **Steam:** Steaming vegetables retains nutrients and delivers a crisp-tender texture.
- **Hydrolyze:** Water breaks down complex molecules, creating rich broths with deep flavors.

Cooking with Water:

Water is utilized in a variety of cooking techniques, each highlighting its unique properties:

- **Poaching:** This gentle cooking method involves simmering food in water just below boiling point. It's ideal for delicate proteins like fish, eggs, and chicken breasts.
- **Simmering:** Simmering involves maintaining a gentle bubbling in the water, perfect for braising meats, stewing vegetables, and creating flavorful soups and sauces.
- **Braising:** This technique combines slow cooking with liquid (often water with added flavorings) to tenderize tougher cuts of meat and infuse them with rich flavors.
- **Broth and Stock Making:** Water acts as the foundation for creating flavorful broths and stocks. Simmering bones, vegetables, and herbs in water extracts their essence, resulting in a concentrated and nourishing base for soups, stews, and sauces.

The following ten recipes will showcase the diverse ways water interacts with food, highlighting its transformative power in the kitchen. Get ready to explore the essence of Water and create dishes that are not only delicious but also embody its nurturing and adaptable spirit.

Salmon's Embrace: A Watery Sanctuary with a Touch of Fire (Poached Salmon with Lemon Dill Sauce)

THIS RECIPE INVITES you to experience the comforting essence of Water. Delicate salmon fillets are gently poached in a simmering broth, showcasing Water's nurturing touch. A vibrant lemon dill sauce adds a refreshing burst of flavor, while the variation offers a touch of Fire with a pinch of cayenne pepper.

Ingredients:

● **Salmon's Embrace (serves 2):**

○ 2 (6-ounce) salmon fillets (skin-on or skinless, your preference)

○ 2 cups (480ml) low-sodium chicken broth or vegetable broth (Water's Foundation)

○ 1 medium onion, sliced

○ 1 lemon, sliced

○ 4 whole black peppercorns

○ 2 sprigs fresh thyme (optional)

○ Salt, to taste

- **Lemon Dill Sauce:**

  ○ 1/4 cup (60ml) unsalted butter
  ○ 2 tablespoons (30ml) chopped fresh dill
  ○ 1 tablespoon (15ml) lemon juice
  ○ Salt and freshly ground black pepper, to taste

- **Variation: A Touch of Fire**

  ○ Pinch of cayenne pepper (optional)

Conversions:
- 1 cup = 240 ml (US customary) or 250 ml (metric)
- 1 tablespoon = 15 ml
- 1 ounce = 28g

Tips:
- Choose fresh, firm salmon fillets for the best results.
- Using a pot with a lid helps maintain a consistent simmer.
- Don't overcrowd the pot. Poach the salmon in a single layer for even cooking.
- Avoid overcooking the fish. Aim for an opaque interior with a slight flakiness.

Allergy/Diet Differences:
- **Vegetarian:** Omit the salmon and use vegetable broth for a flavorful vegetarian poaching liquid. Consider poaching vegetables like asparagus, broccoli, or carrots for a vegetarian main course.
- **Vegan:** Use vegetable broth and a vegan butter substitute for the sauce. Opt for fresh herbs like parsley or chives instead of dill for a vegan option.
- **Gluten-free:** This recipe is naturally gluten-free.

Instructions:

Poaching the Salmon:

1. In a large pot, combine the chicken or vegetable broth, onion, lemon slices, peppercorns, thyme sprigs (if using), and a pinch of salt. Bring to a simmer over medium heat.
2. Gently place the salmon fillets in the simmering broth. Cover the pot and reduce heat to low.
3. Poach the salmon for 8-10 minutes, or until just cooked through and opaque in the center. The exact cooking time may vary depending on the thickness of the fillets.

Lemon Dill Sauce:

1. While the salmon poaches, melt the butter in a small saucepan over medium heat.

2. Add the dill and lemon juice to the melted butter. Cook for 1 minute, stirring constantly, to release the flavors.
3. Season the sauce with salt and pepper to taste.

Serving Suggestions:

1. Carefully transfer the poached salmon fillets to plates.
2. Spoon the lemon dill sauce over the salmon.
3. Garnish with a lemon wedge and fresh dill sprigs (optional).

Variation: A Touch of Fire

● For a touch of Fire, add a pinch of cayenne pepper to the lemon dill sauce while it simmers. Adjust the amount based on your desired level of spice.

With this recipe, you've embraced the essence of Water. The gentle poaching method preserves the salmon's delicate texture, while the lemon dill sauce adds a refreshing touch. The optional hint of cayenne pepper from the variation introduces a fiery element, demonstrating the beautiful interplay of Water and Fire. Enjoy this dish, savoring the nurturing embrace of Water and the vibrant flavors it brings to life!

A Garden in a Bowl: Water's Bounty Meets Earth's Embrace (Creamy Tomato Pasta with Fresh Herbs)

THIS RECIPE INVITES you to celebrate the harmonious union of Water and Earth. Fresh, vibrant tomatoes, representing Water's essence, are transformed into a silky sauce, while the addition of creamy cheese and fresh herbs embodies Earth's richness. A variation offers an opportunity to incorporate earthy elements with sun-dried tomatoes, adding a deeper layer of flavor.

Ingredients (Basic Recipe):

● **Water's Bounty:**

○ 1 (28-ounce) can crushed tomatoes

○ 1/2 cup (120ml) low-sodium chicken broth or vegetable broth

○ 1 tablespoon olive oil

- **Earth's Embrace:**

  ○ 1 pound (450g) dry pasta (such as penne, farfalle, or rotini)
  ○ 1/2 cup (113g) mascarpone cheese or ricotta cheese
  ○ 1/4 cup (50g) grated Parmesan cheese
  ○ 1/4 cup (4g) chopped fresh basil
  ○ 1/4 cup (4g) chopped fresh parsley
  ○ Salt and freshly ground black pepper, to taste

- **Optional Equipment:**

  ○ Immersion blender (for a smoother sauce)

Conversions:
- 1 cup = 240 ml (US customary) or 250 ml (metric)
- 1 tablespoon = 15 ml
- 1 pound = 450g

Tips:
- Use high-quality crushed tomatoes for the best flavor.
- Reserve some pasta water before draining. This starchy water helps create a silky sauce when incorporated.
- Don't overcook the pasta. Aim for al dente, which means cooked to the tooth with a slight bite.

Allergy/Diet Differences:
- **Vegetarian:** This recipe is naturally vegetarian.
- **Vegan:** Use vegetable broth and omit the cheese. Opt for a vegan Parmesan cheese substitute or nutritional yeast for a cheesy flavor. Choose vegan butter or olive oil for sauteing.
- **Gluten-free:** Use gluten-free pasta. Ensure all other ingredients are certified gluten-free.

Instructions:

Water's Bounty:

1. In a large pot or Dutch oven, heat the olive oil over medium heat.

Earth's Embrace (Basic Recipe):

1. Add the crushed tomatoes, chicken or vegetable broth, and a pinch of salt to the hot olive oil. Bring to a simmer and cook for 15 minutes, stirring occasionally, to allow the flavors to meld.

Cooking the Pasta:

1. While the sauce simmers, bring a large pot of salted water to a boil. Add the pasta and cook according to package instructions for al dente. Reserve 1/2 cup of the pasta water before draining.

Creamy Bliss:

1. Once the sauce has simmered for 15 minutes, remove the pot from the heat. Stir in the mascarpone or ricotta cheese, Parmesan cheese, chopped basil, and chopped parsley. Season with salt and pepper to taste.
2. If desired, use an immersion blender to achieve a smoother sauce consistency. Alternatively, you can puree a

portion of the sauce in a blender and then return it to the pot.

3. Add the drained pasta to the pot with the sauce. Toss gently to coat the pasta evenly. If the sauce seems too thick, gradually add some of the reserved pasta water until you reach a desired consistency.

Serving Suggestions:

1. Serve the creamy tomato pasta with fresh basil leaves or chopped parsley as garnish (optional).

Variation: Incorporate Earthy Elements with Sun-Dried Tomatoes

● Before adding the crushed tomatoes to the pot in step 1, rehydrate 5-6 sun-dried tomatoes in hot water for 10 minutes. Chop them finely and saute them in the olive oil along with a clove of minced garlic for a minute before adding the crushed tomatoes and broth. This variation adds a deeper, earthier flavor to the sauce.

With this recipe, you've brought Water and Earth together in a delightful dance. The vibrant tomato sauce, representing Water's essence, embraces the richness of cheese and herbs, embodying Earth's bounty. The optional sun-dried tomatoes in the variation add another layer of earthiness, showcasing the versatility of this dish. Enjoy this flavorful creation, savoring the harmonious union of the elements!

A Fisherman's Bounty: A Symphony of Water and Fire (Seafood Cioppino)

THIS RECIPE INVITES you to experience the magic that unfolds when Water meets Fire. Fresh seafood, representing the essence of Water, simmers in a vibrant tomato broth, infused with the transformative kiss of Fire. This cioppino is a celebration of the bounty of the sea, perfect for a special occasion or a comforting weeknight meal.

Ingredients:

● **Water's Bounty (approximately 1½ pounds total seafood):**

○ 1 pound (450g) mussels, debearded and scrubbed

○ 1 pound (450g) clams, scrubbed well

○ ½ pound (225g) shrimp, peeled and deveined

○ ½ pound (225g) cod fillets, cut into bite-sized pieces

○ ½ pound (225g) sea scallops

○ (Optional) ¼ pound (113g) calamari rings or tentacles, cleaned and sliced

- **Fire's Embrace (Broth):**

○ 1 tablespoon olive oil
○ 1 onion, diced
○ 2 cloves garlic, minced
○ 1 (28-ounce) can crushed tomatoes
○ 1 (14.5-ounce) can diced tomatoes (undrained)
○ 1 cup (240ml) dry white wine
○ 1 cup (240ml) fish stock or vegetable broth
○ 1 bay leaf
○ 1 teaspoon dried oregano
○ ½ teaspoon dried thyme
○ Pinch of red pepper flakes (optional)
○ Salt and freshly ground black pepper, to taste

- **Finishing Touches:**

○ ¼ cup (60ml) chopped fresh parsley
○ Crusty bread, for serving (optional)

Conversions:
- 1 cup = 240 ml (US customary) or 250 ml (metric)
- 1 tablespoon = 15 ml
- 1 pound = 450g

Tips:
- Use fresh, high-quality seafood for the best flavor.
- Ensure the mussels and clams are tightly closed before adding them to the pot. Discard any that are open and don't close when tapped.
- Don't overcook the seafood. It cooks quickly and can become tough if overcooked.

Allergy/Diet Differences:
- **Pescatarian:** This recipe is naturally pescatarian.
- **Shellfish allergy:** Omit the mussels and clams. Adjust the cooking time for the remaining seafood based on their individual cooking needs.
- **Gluten-free:** This recipe is naturally gluten-free. Ensure all ingredients are certified gluten-free if necessary.

Instructions:

Fire's Embrace (Broth):

1. In a large Dutch oven or heavy-bottomed pot, heat the olive oil over medium heat. Add the diced onion and cook until softened, about 5 minutes.
2. Stir in the minced garlic and cook for an additional minute, until fragrant.
3. Add the crushed tomatoes, diced tomatoes (with their juices), white wine, fish stock or vegetable broth, bay

leaf, oregano, thyme, and red pepper flakes (if using). Season with salt and pepper to taste. Bring to a simmer and cook for 15 minutes, allowing the flavors to meld.

Water's Bounty:

1. Increase the heat to medium-high. Add the mussels and clams to the simmering broth. Cover the pot and cook for 5-7 minutes, or until the mussels and clams open. Discard any mussels or clams that remain unopened.
2. Add the shrimp, cod fillets, and sea scallops (and calamari, if using) to the pot. Gently stir to combine. Cover again and cook for an additional 3-5 minutes, or until the shrimp are pink and opaque, the cod is cooked through and flaky, and the scallops are just seared on the outside.

Finishing Touches:

1. Stir in the chopped fresh parsley. Taste and adjust seasonings as needed.
2. Serve the cioppino immediately in bowls with crusty bread for dipping (optional).

With this recipe, you've become an alchemist, transforming the bounty of the sea and the power of Fire into a heartwarming cioppino. The vibrant broth, representing Water's essence, embraces the delicate seafood, showcasing a delightful dance of the elements. Enjoy this flavorful dish, savoring the taste of the ocean and the magic it brings to your table!

A Symphony of Water and Earth: Vegetable Broth with Dumplings (Variation: Embrace Air with Wonton Wrappers)

THIS RECIPE INVITES you to explore the harmonious union of Water and Earth. A soul-warming vegetable broth, embodying Water's nurturing essence, is enriched with savory dumplings, representing Earth's bounty. The variation offers an opportunity to incorporate the element of Air with delicate wonton wrappers, creating a delightful textural contrast.

Ingredients (Basic Recipe):

● **Water's Embrace (Broth):**

  ○ 8 cups (2 liters) water
  ○ 1 tablespoon olive oil
  ○ 1 onion, chopped
  ○ 2 carrots, chopped

- ○ 2 celery stalks, chopped
- ○ 2 cloves garlic, minced
- ○ 1 teaspoon dried thyme
- ○ 1 bay leaf
- ○ Salt and freshly ground black pepper, to taste

- ● **Earth's Bounty (Dumplings):**

- ○ 1 cup (120g) all-purpose flour
- ○ ½ teaspoon salt
- ○ ½ cup (120ml) boiling water
- ○ Vegetable filling (see suggestions below)

Vegetable Filling Suggestions:
- ● 1 cup (150g) shredded cabbage, mixed with 1/4 cup (60ml) chopped mushrooms and 1 tablespoon soy sauce
- ● 1 cup (150g) chopped tofu, crumbled, mixed with 1 tablespoon chopped scallions, 1 tablespoon grated ginger, and 1 teaspoon sesame oil
- ● 1 cup (150g) grated potatoes, mixed with 1/4 cup (60ml) chopped cooked vegetables (such as peas, carrots, or corn) and 1/4 teaspoon dried dill

Conversions:
- ● 1 cup = 240 ml (US customary) or 250 ml (metric)
- ● 1 tablespoon = 15 ml

Tips:
- ● Use a variety of vegetables for the broth to create a richer flavor.
- ● For the dumplings, ensure the boiling water is poured all at once to create a pliable dough.
- ● Don't overwork the dumpling dough. A few lumps are okay.
- ● The dumplings can be cooked ahead of time and stored in the refrigerator for up to 2 days. Reheat them in the simmering broth.

Allergy/Diet Differences:
- ● **Vegan:** Use vegetable broth and a vegan filling for the dumplings. Opt for gluten-free flour if needed.
- ● **Gluten-free:** Use a gluten-free flour blend for the dumplings. Ensure all other ingredients are certified gluten-free.

Instructions:

Water's Embrace (Broth):

1. In a large pot, heat the olive oil over medium heat. Add the chopped onion, carrots, and celery. Cook until softened, about 5 minutes.
2. Stir in the garlic, thyme, and bay leaf. Cook for an additional minute, until fragrant.
3. Add the water and bring to a boil. Reduce heat to low and simmer for 30 minutes, allowing the flavors to develop.
4. Season the broth with salt and pepper to taste. Strain the broth if desired, removing the vegetables.

Earth's Bounty (Dumplings - Basic Recipe):

1. In a large bowl, whisk together the flour and salt.

2. Slowly add the boiling water to the flour mixture, stirring with a fork until a shaggy dough forms.
3. Knead the dough on a lightly floured surface for 2-3 minutes, or until smooth and elastic. Cover the dough with plastic wrap and let it rest for 15 minutes.

Assemble the Dumplings:

1. On a lightly floured surface, roll out the dough to a thin sheet (about 1/16 inch thick).
2. Using a round cookie cutter or a glass, cut out circles from the dough.
3. Place a spoonful of your chosen vegetable filling in the center of each dough circle.
4. Moisten the edges of the dough circle with water. Fold the dough over the filling to form a half-moon shape. Pinch the edges to seal the dumpling.

Cooking the Dumplings:

1. Bring the vegetable broth back to a simmer.
2. Gently drop the dumplings into the simmering broth. Cook for 5-7 minutes, or until they float to the surface and become cooked through.

Serving Suggestions:

1. Ladle the vegetable broth with dumplings into bowls.
2. Garnish with chopped fresh herbs like parsley or chives (optional).
3. Serve with a side of crusty bread (optional).

Variation: Embrace Air with Wonton Wrappers

1. Instead of making your own dough, use store-bought wonton wrappers. These thin and delicate wrappers, representing the element of Air, create a delightful textural contrast with the savory broth and dumplings.
2. Follow the same instructions for assembling the dumplings (placing a spoonful of filling in the center and folding the dough over). However, due to the wonton wrappers' thinner nature, you may not need to moisten the edges before sealing. Simply pinch the edges firmly to create a tight seal.
3. Cook the wonton dumplings in the simmering broth for 3-4 minutes, or until they become translucent and cooked through.

With this recipe, you've celebrated the harmonious union of Water and Earth. The soul-warming vegetable broth, embodying Water's essence, is enriched with the dumplings, representing Earth's bounty. The optional variation with wonton wrappers adds a touch of Air, showcasing the beautiful interplay of the elements on your plate. Enjoy this comforting and flavorful dish, savoring the taste of the earth nourished by water and the gentle influence of air!

A Gift from the Earth: Lemony Lentil Soup with a Touch of Air (Lentil Soup with Lemon and Fresh Herbs)

This recipe invites you to celebrate the humble lentil, a symbol of Earth's bounty. A hearty and nourishing soup, brimming with protein and fiber, is infused with the refreshing brightness of lemon and the fragrant touch of fresh herbs. The inclusion of fresh herbs at the end adds a touch of Air, bringing a vibrant finish to the dish.

Ingredients:

● **Earth's Bounty:**

- 1 tablespoon olive oil
- 1 onion, chopped
- 2 carrots, chopped
- 2 celery stalks, chopped
- 2 cloves garlic, minced
- 1 teaspoon ground cumin
- ½ teaspoon ground coriander
- Pinch of red pepper flakes (optional)
- 1 cup (200g) green lentils, rinsed and picked over
- 8 cups (2 liters) vegetable broth or chicken broth

- **Water's Embrace:**

  - 1 (14.5-ounce) can diced tomatoes, undrained

- **Spirit's Kiss (Lemon and Herbs):**

  - Zest and juice of 1 lemon
  - ¼ cup (4g) chopped fresh parsley
  - ¼ cup (4g) chopped fresh dill
  - Salt and freshly ground black pepper, to taste

Conversions:
- 1 cup = 240 ml (US customary) or 250 ml (metric)
- 1 tablespoon = 15 ml

Tips:
- Use a variety of fresh herbs for a more complex flavor profile. Options include basil, oregano, or thyme.
- Don't overcook the lentils. They should be tender but still retain their shape.
- Adjust the amount of lemon juice to your desired level of tartness.

Allergy/Diet Differences:
- **Vegetarian:** This recipe is naturally vegetarian.
- **Vegan:** Use vegetable broth and omit any dairy products served alongside the soup (such as a dollop of yogurt).
- **Gluten-free:** This recipe is naturally gluten-free.

Instructions:

Earth's Bounty:

1. In a large pot or Dutch oven, heat the olive oil over medium heat. Add the chopped onion, carrots, and celery. Cook until softened, about 5 minutes.
2. Stir in the garlic, cumin, coriander, and red pepper flakes (if using). Cook for an additional minute, until fragrant.
3. Add the rinsed lentils and vegetable or chicken broth. Bring to a boil, then reduce heat to low and simmer for 20-25 minutes, or until the lentils are tender.

Water's Embrace:

1. Stir in the diced tomatoes with their juices. Simmer for an additional 5 minutes, allowing the flavors to meld.

Spirit's Kiss (Lemon and Herbs):

1. Just before serving, stir in the lemon zest and juice. Season with salt and pepper to taste.
2. Remove the pot from the heat and stir in the chopped fresh parsley and dill.

Serving Suggestions:

1. Ladle the lentil soup into bowls.
2. Garnish with additional chopped fresh herbs (optional).
3. Serve with crusty bread for dipping (optional).

With this recipe, you've transformed the humble lentil into a nourishing and flavorful dish. Earth's bounty shines through with every spoonful, embraced by the gentle touch of Water in the broth. The final addition of fresh herbs adds a touch of Air, leaving a refreshing finish that uplifts the spirit. Enjoy this heartwarming soup, savoring the magic of the elements on your plate!

Earth and Water: Poached Eggs on Avocado Toast (Variation: Embrace Earth's Embrace with Whole-Grain Toast)

THIS RECIPE INVITES you to celebrate a harmonious union of Earth and Water. Luscious avocado, representing Earth's richness, is transformed into a creamy spread for toast, while perfectly poached eggs, symbolic of Water's essence, bring a touch of decadence. The variation offers an opportunity to incorporate earthy elements with whole-grain toast, adding depth and texture to the dish.

Ingredients:

● **Earth's Bounty:**

○ 2 slices bread (your choice: white, wheat, or sourdough)

○ 1 ripe avocado

○ Salt and freshly ground black pepper, to taste

○ (Optional for Variation) 2 slices whole-grain bread

- **Water's Embrace (Poached Eggs):**

  ○ 2 large eggs
  ○ 2 tablespoons (30ml) white vinegar or apple cider vinegar
  ○ Pinch of salt

Conversions:
- 1 tablespoon = 15 ml

Tips:
- Use the freshest, ripest avocados for the creamiest texture.
- For perfectly poached eggs, ensure your water simmers gently and not at a rolling boil.
- Don't overcrowd the pot when poaching eggs. Poach them one or two at a time for the best results.

Allergy/Diet Differences:
- **Vegetarian:** This recipe is naturally vegetarian.
- **Vegan:** Opt for a vegan butter substitute or mashed chickpeas instead of avocado spread. Ensure the bread is vegan-friendly.
- **Gluten-free:** Choose gluten-free bread. Ensure all other ingredients are certified gluten-free.

Instructions:

Earth's Bounty:

1. Toast the bread slices to your desired level of crispness.
2. While the bread toasts, cut the avocado in half, remove the pit, and scoop the flesh into a bowl. Mash the avocado with a fork until creamy. Season with salt and pepper to taste.

Water's Embrace (Poached Eggs):

1. Fill a medium saucepan with about 2-3 inches of water. Add the vinegar or apple cider vinegar and a pinch of salt. Bring the water to a simmer (gentle bubbles).

2. **Two Methods for Poaching Eggs:**

  ○ **Swirling Method:** Create a gentle whirlpool in the simmering water by stirring it with a spoon. Crack an egg into a small bowl or ramekin. Once the water is swirling, gently tip the egg from the bowl close to the center of the whirlpool. The swirling water will help shape the egg white. Repeat with the second egg, ensuring there's enough space between them. Poach the eggs for 3-4 minutes for runny yolks, or slightly longer for firmer yolks.

  ○ **Spoon Method:** Crack each egg into a small bowl or ramekin. Gently lower the eggs, one at a time, into the simmering water using a spoon. Poach for 3-4 minutes for runny yolks, or slightly longer for firmer yolks.

3. Once poached, use a slotted spoon to remove the eggs from the water and drain any excess liquid.

Assemble the Toast:

1. Spread the mashed avocado on the toasted bread slices.
2. Gently place a poached egg on top of each avocado toast.
3. Season with additional salt and pepper (optional).

Variation: Embrace Earth's Embrace with Whole-Grain Toast

● Substitute the white, wheat, or sourdough bread with whole-grain toast for a deeper flavor and added fiber. The earthy texture of whole grains complements the creamy avocado and the richness of the poached egg, creating a delightful textural experience.

Serving Suggestions:

● Serve the avocado toast with poached eggs immediately.

● Garnish with a sprinkle of red pepper flakes, chopped fresh herbs (such as chives or cilantro), or a drizzle of hot sauce (optional).

With this recipe, you've created a beautiful harmony between Earth and Water. The creamy avocado toast, representing Earth's bounty, is the perfect canvas for the luxurious poached eggs, embodying Water's essence. The optional variation with whole-grain bread adds another layer of earthiness, showcasing the versatility of this dish. Enjoy this simple yet elegant breakfast or brunch option, savoring the interplay of the elements on your plate!

Gift from the Earth, Kissed by Fire: Creamy Mushroom Risotto (Risotto ai Funghi)

THIS RECIPE INVITES you to celebrate the humble mushroom, a treasure of the Earth. Earthy and flavorful mushrooms are transformed into a creamy risotto, a dish that embodies the nurturing essence of Water and the transformative kiss of Fire. As you stir the rice, releasing its starches and creating a luxuriously smooth texture, you become an alchemist in the kitchen.

Ingredients:

- **Earth's Bounty (Mushrooms):**

  ○ 1 tablespoon olive oil

  ○ 1 onion, finely chopped

  ○ 1 clove garlic, minced

○ 1 pound (450g) mixed mushrooms, sliced (such as cremini, portobello, shiitake)

○ ½ cup (120ml) dry white wine (optional)

○ ½ cup (113g) grated Parmesan cheese, plus additional for garnish (optional)

○ Salt and freshly ground black pepper, to taste

● **Water's Embrace (Broth):**

○ 4 cups (1 liter) vegetable broth or chicken broth, warmed

● **Air's Kiss (Rice):**

○ 1½ cups (300g) Arborio rice

● **Fire's Touch (Butter):**

○ 2 tablespoons (28g) unsalted butter

Conversions:
● 1 cup = 240 ml (US customary) or 250 ml (metric)
● 1 tablespoon = 15 ml
● 1 pound = 450g
Tips:
● Use a variety of mushrooms for a more complex flavor profile.
● Toasting the rice in the beginning helps develop a nutty flavor.
● Gradual addition of warm broth allows the rice to release its starches and achieve a creamy texture.
● Don't overcook the rice. Aim for al dente, with a slight bite in the center.
Allergy/Diet Differences:
● **Vegetarian:** This recipe is naturally vegetarian.
● **Vegan:** Use vegetable broth and omit the cheese. Opt for a vegan Parmesan cheese substitute or nutritional yeast for a cheesy flavor. Choose vegan butter or olive oil for sauteing.
● **Gluten-free:** Use certified gluten-free Arborio rice. Ensure all other ingredients are certified gluten-free.
Instructions:
Earth's Bounty (Mushrooms):

1. In a large saucepan or Dutch oven, heat the olive oil over medium heat. Add the chopped onion and cook until softened, about 5 minutes.
2. Stir in the minced garlic and cook for an additional minute, until fragrant.
3. Add the sliced mushrooms and cook for 5-7 minutes, or until softened and golden brown. Season with salt and pepper to taste.

Water's Embrace (Broth):

1. While the mushrooms cook, warm the vegetable or chicken broth in a separate pot or saucepan. Keep it simmering on low heat.

Air's Kiss (Rice) and Fire's Touch (Butter):

1. Add the Arborio rice to the pan with the cooked mushrooms. Stir to coat the rice with the oil. Toast the rice for 1-2 minutes, stirring constantly.
2. Add the white wine (if using) and cook, stirring constantly, until the wine is absorbed.
3. Gradually add the warmed broth, about ½ cup at a time, stirring constantly after each addition. Allow the rice to absorb the broth before adding more. Continue this process until all the broth is used, and the rice is cooked through but still has a slight bite in the center (al dente). This will take approximately 18-20 minutes.
4. Once the rice is cooked, remove the pan from the heat. Stir in the butter and Parmesan cheese (if using). Season with additional salt and pepper to taste.

Serving Suggestions:

1. Spoon the creamy mushroom risotto into plates.
2. Garnish with additional grated Parmesan cheese (optional) and a sprinkle of chopped fresh herbs like parsley or chives (optional).

With this recipe, you've become an alchemist, transforming the humble mushroom into a delightful and comforting dish. The earthiness of the mushrooms shines through, embraced by the creamy texture achieved through the gentle addition of Water's essence. The final touch of butter adds a hint of Fire's kiss, creating a symphony of flavors on your plate. Enjoy this culinary creation, savoring the magic you've woven in the kitchen!

Earth Meets Water with a Touch of Fire (Coconut Curry with Vegetables or Tofu)

THIS RECIPE INVITES you to embark on a culinary adventure to the tropics. Fragrant vegetables or pan-fried tofu, representing Earth's bounty, simmer in a creamy coconut curry, a vibrant dance between Water's essence and the warmth of Fire. The variation offers an opportunity to add fiery elements with red curry paste, igniting your taste buds with a touch of heat.

Ingredients:

● **Earth's Bounty (Vegetables or Tofu):**

  ○ 1 tablespoon olive oil

  ○ 1 onion, chopped

  ○ 2 cloves garlic, minced

○ 1 (14.5-ounce) can diced tomatoes, undrained

○ 1 cup (240ml) vegetable broth

○ 1 (13.5-ounce) can coconut milk (full-fat)

○ 1-2 tablespoons curry powder (depending on desired spice level)

○ 1 tablespoon soy sauce

○ 1 tablespoon brown sugar

○ 1-2 cups chopped vegetables (such as broccoli, bell peppers, carrots, green beans)

○ (Optional) 1 block (14 ounces) firm tofu, drained and cubed

● **Water's Embrace (Finishing Touches):**

○ Salt and freshly ground black pepper, to taste
○ Fresh lime juice, to taste
○ Chopped fresh cilantro, for garnish (optional)

● **Variation: Add Fiery Elements with Red Curry Paste**

○ 1-2 tablespoons red curry paste (depending on desired spice level)

Conversions:
● 1 cup = 240 ml (US customary) or 250 ml (metric)
● 1 tablespoon = 15 ml
Tips:
● Use a variety of colorful vegetables for added visual appeal and flavor.
● If using tofu, pan-fry it until golden brown on all sides before adding it to the curry.
● Adjust the amount of curry powder and red curry paste (in the variation) to your desired level of spice.
Allergy/Diet Differences:
● **Vegetarian:** This recipe is naturally vegetarian.
● **Vegan:** Use vegetable broth and coconut milk and omit the optional soy sauce. Ensure the curry powder is vegan-friendly.
● **Gluten-free:** Ensure all ingredients are certified gluten-free.
Instructions:
Earth's Bounty (Vegetables or Tofu):

1. In a large pot or Dutch oven, heat the olive oil over medium heat. Add the chopped onion and cook until softened, about 5 minutes.
2. Stir in the minced garlic and cook for an additional minute, until fragrant.

Water's Embrace (Base of the Curry):

1. Add the diced tomatoes with their juices, vegetable broth, coconut milk, curry powder, soy sauce (if not using a vegan option), and brown sugar. Bring to a simmer and cook for 10 minutes, allowing the flavors to meld.

Earth's Bounty (Vegetables):

1. If using vegetables, add them to the simmering curry and cook for 5-7 minutes, or until tender-crisp.

Earth's Bounty (Tofu - Optional):

1. If using tofu, pan-fry it in a separate pan with a little oil until golden brown on all sides. Then, add the pan-fried tofu to the simmering curry.

Simmering and Finishing Touches:

1. Season the curry with salt and pepper to taste. Add a squeeze of fresh lime juice for a touch of acidity.
2. Simmer for an additional 2-3 minutes to allow the flavors to further develop.

Variation: Add Fiery Elements with Red Curry Paste
● Before adding the diced tomatoes in step 3, stir in 1-2 tablespoons of red curry paste depending on your desired spice level. This adds a fiery element to the curry, showcasing the transformative kiss of Fire.
Serving Suggestions:

1. Ladle the coconut curry with vegetables or tofu into bowls.
2. Garnish with chopped fresh cilantro (optional) and serve with rice or naan bread.

With this recipe, you've embarked on a culinary adventure. The vibrant vegetables or tofu, representing Earth's bounty, simmer in a creamy coconut curry, a delightful dance between Water's essence and the warmth of Fire. The optional red curry paste in the variation adds a fiery element, showcasing the beautiful interplay of the elements on your plate. Enjoy this flavorful and exotic dish, savoring the taste of the tropics!

A Symphony of Water and Air: Summer Fruit Soup with Mint and Yogurt (Gazpacho de Frutas)

THIS RECIPE INVITES you to celebrate the vibrant spirit of summer. Fresh, seasonal fruits, representing the essence of Water, are transformed into a refreshing and chilled soup. A touch of Air is incorporated with fresh mint leaves, adding a fragrant and uplifting note. Creamy yogurt brings a touch of richness and body, creating a symphony of flavors and textures on your palate.

Ingredients:

● **Water's Bounty (Fruit):**

○ 4 cups (600g) mixed seasonal fruits (such as strawberries, blueberries, raspberries, peaches, melon)

○ ½ cup (120ml) orange juice

○ ¼ cup (60ml) fresh lime juice

- **Air's Kiss (Mint):**

  o ¼ cup (packed) fresh mint leaves, plus additional for garnish

- **Spirit's Touch (Yogurt and Sweetener):**

  o ½ cup (120ml) plain yogurt (whole milk, low-fat, or Greek yogurt)
  o 2 tablespoons honey or maple syrup (adjust to taste)

Conversions:
- 1 cup = 240 ml (US customary) or 250 ml (metric)
- ¼ cup = 60 ml
- ½ cup = 120 ml

Tips:
- Use a variety of ripe and flavorful fruits for the best results. Frozen fruits can be used, but thaw them completely before blending.
- Adjust the amount of orange juice and lime juice to your desired level of sweetness and tartness.
- For a smoother texture, strain the soup after blending.

Allergy/Diet Differences:
- **Vegan:** Use plant-based yogurt and omit the honey or maple syrup. Opt for a natural sweetener like agave nectar or dates.
- **Dairy-free:** Use dairy-free yogurt or coconut yogurt. Opt for a plant-based milk alternative (such as almond milk or coconut milk) instead of yogurt for a thinner soup.

Instructions:

Water's Bounty (Fruit):

1. Wash and chop the seasonal fruits into bite-sized pieces.

Air's Kiss (Mint):

1. Set aside a few mint leaves for garnish. Add the remaining mint leaves to a blender along with the chopped fruits, orange juice, and lime juice.

Spirit's Touch (Yogurt and Sweetener):

1. Add the yogurt and honey or maple syrup to the blender.

Blending and Finishing Touches:

1. Blend until smooth. Taste and adjust the sweetness and tartness by adding more honey/maple syrup, orange juice, or lime juice as desired.
2. Chill the soup in the refrigerator for at least 30 minutes before serving.

Serving Suggestions:

1. Ladle the chilled summer fruit soup into bowls.

2. Garnish with a dollop of yogurt (optional) and the reserved fresh mint leaves.

With this recipe, you've become an alchemist in your kitchen. Fresh, seasonal fruits, representing Water's essence, are transformed into a refreshing soup. The fragrant touch of mint leaves adds a touch of Air, creating a delightful dance on your palate. The creamy yogurt brings a touch of richness, and the final chill brings a refreshing coolness. Enjoy this vibrant and flavorful soup, savoring the taste of summer captured in every spoonful!

Water and Earth: Watercress and Cucumber Salad with a Light Vinaigrette

THIS RECIPE INVITES you to experience the refreshing harmony between Water and Earth. Crisp watercress, symbolizing Water's essence, is paired with cool cucumber, representing Earth's bounty. A light vinaigrette ties the elements together, creating a vibrant and healthy salad perfect for a summer side dish or a light lunch.

Ingredients:

- **Water's Essence (Watercress):**

○ 2 bunches watercress, rinsed and patted dry

● **Earth's Bounty (Cucumber):**

○ 1 large English cucumber, thinly sliced (about ¼ inch thick)

● **Spirit's Kiss (Vinaigrette):**

○ 2 tablespoons olive oil
○ 1 tablespoon white wine vinegar or lemon juice
○ 1 teaspoon Dijon mustard
○ ½ teaspoon honey or maple syrup (optional)
○ Salt and freshly ground black pepper, to taste

Conversions:
● 1 tablespoon = 15 ml
Tips:
● Choose a fresh, crisp cucumber for the best results.
● If the watercress has thick stems, remove them before adding the leaves to the salad.
● For a more flavorful vinaigrette, whisk in a pinch of dried herbs like dill or oregano.
Allergy/Diet Differences:
● **Vegan:** This recipe is naturally vegan.
● **Gluten-free:** This recipe is naturally gluten-free.
Instructions:
Water's Essence (Watercress):

1. Wash the watercress thoroughly and pat it dry with a paper towel.

Earth's Bounty (Cucumber):

1. Thinly slice the cucumber. You can use a mandoline slicer for even slices or slice them by hand.

Spirit's Kiss (Vinaigrette):

1. In a small bowl, whisk together the olive oil, vinegar or lemon juice, Dijon mustard, and honey or maple syrup (if using). Season with salt and pepper to taste.

Assembling the Salad:

1. In a large bowl, combine the watercress and cucumber slices.
2. Toss the salad with the prepared vinaigrette just before serving.

Serving Suggestions:

1. Serve the watercress and cucumber salad immediately.
2. For an extra touch of elegance, garnish with a sprinkle of crumbled feta cheese or chopped fresh herbs (optional).

With this recipe, you've created a symphony of Water and Earth. The crisp watercress, symbolizing Water's essence, is perfectly complemented by the cool cucumber, representing Earth's bounty. The light vinaigrette brings the elements together, creating a refreshing and flavorful salad. Enjoy this healthy and satisfying dish, savoring the interplay of the elements on your plate!

Part 5: Spirit (10 Recipes)

Welcome to the realm of Spirit! This section delves into the essence of creativity, intuition, and the transformative power that lies within us all. Here, we move beyond the foundation of the elements and explore the boundless possibilities of culinary alchemy.

Essence of Spirit:

Spirit embodies the spark of inspiration, the dance between intuition and knowledge, and the transformative power that elevates a dish from mere sustenance to an artistic expression. It's the playful experimentation, the unexpected flavor pairings, and the artistic presentation that elevate the dining experience.

Cooking with Spirit:

In this section, we'll explore unconventional techniques, delve into exciting flavor combinations, and experiment with plating presentations that go beyond the ordinary. Get ready to:

● **Embrace Smoke and Infusion:** We'll explore smoking techniques, both hot and cold, to add a touch of mystery and depth to your dishes. We'll also delve into the world of infusions, where unexpected ingredients like herbs, teas, and even woodsmoke can transform simple dishes.

● **Deconstruct and Reconstruct:** Let's break down classic dishes and reimagine them with a playful twist. We'll explore plating techniques that challenge the norm and encourage you to see food as an artistic canvas.

● **Embrace Unexpected Pairings:** Forget the tried and true! We'll take you on a journey of flavor exploration, where sweet meets savory, and familiar ingredients find new partners in crime.

Through these ten recipes, you'll unlock the power of Spirit in the kitchen. Get ready to unleash your creativity, trust your intuition, and transform your culinary repertoire into an expression of your unique spirit!

Deconstructed Sushi Bowls

WELCOME TO THE REALM of Spirit, where we embrace playfulness and creativity! This recipe takes the classic sushi roll and deconstructs it into a vibrant bowl, allowing you to customize your experience. Let your intuition guide you as you choose your favorite ingredients, unleashing your inner sushi artist.

Ingredients:

Foundation (Choose your favorites):

● **Earth's Bounty (Grains and Vegetables):**

○ 1 cup (200g) cooked sushi rice (white, brown, or black)

○ 1 cup (150g) shredded vegetables (such as carrots, cucumbers, radishes, bell peppers)

○ ½ cup (75g) edamame, shelled and cooked (optional)

○ ¼ cup (25g) crumbled seaweed salad (wakame) (optional)

● **Water's Embrace (Protein):**

○ 4 ounces (113g) cooked, flaked fish (such as salmon, tuna, or cod)
○ ½ cup (120ml) cooked, shredded chicken or tofu (optional)
○ ¼ cup (60ml) cooked, crumbled tempeh (optional)

Spirit's Kiss (Flavor and Finish):
● 2 tablespoons soy sauce
● 1 tablespoon rice vinegar
● 1 tablespoon sesame oil
● 1 teaspoon sriracha (optional)
● 1 teaspoon wasabi paste (optional)
● 1 avocado, thinly sliced
● 1 sheet nori seaweed, cut into thin strips
● Pickled ginger, to taste
● Sesame seeds, for garnish

Conversions:
● 1 cup = 240 ml (US customary) or 250 ml (metric)
● 1 tablespoon = 15 ml
● ¼ cup = 60 ml
● ½ cup = 120 ml

Tips:
● Get creative with your ingredients! Leftover roasted vegetables, grilled shrimp, or even kimchi can be added for a unique twist.
● Prepare the sushi rice according to package instructions or your preferred method.
● Marinate the cooked protein (fish, chicken, tofu, or tempeh) in a mixture of soy sauce, rice vinegar, and sesame oil for added flavor (optional).
● Use a cookie cutter to create fun shapes from the avocado slices.

Allergy/Diet Differences:
● **Vegetarian:** Omit the seafood and use tofu, tempeh, or edamame for protein.
● **Vegan:** Use plant-based protein alternatives like tofu, tempeh, or lentils. Opt for vegan versions of soy sauce and mayonnaise (for sriracha). Choose pickled ginger preserved in vinegar instead of brine.
● **Gluten-free:** Ensure all ingredients are certified gluten-free, especially the soy sauce. Consider using tamari, a naturally gluten-free soy sauce substitute.

Instructions:
Building Your Bowl:

1. Divide the cooked sushi rice among individual bowls.
2. Arrange your chosen protein, vegetables, and other toppings on top of the rice.
3. In a small bowl, whisk together the soy sauce, rice vinegar, sesame oil, sriracha (if using), and wasabi paste (if using). Drizzle the dressing over the bowl to your desired amount.

Spirit's Touch:

1. Garnish the bowls with avocado slices, nori strips, pickled ginger, and sesame seeds.

Serving Suggestions:
- Serve the deconstructed sushi bowls immediately.
- Offer additional soy sauce, sriracha, and wasabi paste on the side for individual customization.

Embrace the Spirit!

This recipe is just a starting point. Let your creativity flow and experiment with different flavor combinations and textures. Deconstructed sushi bowls are a delightful way to explore the world of sushi in a playful and personalized manner. Enjoy the process of building your own masterpiece and savor the delicious results!

A Molecular Gastronomy Adventure (Spherification, Foams & Beyond)

WELCOME TO THE REALM of Spirit, where we push boundaries and explore the transformative power of culinary science! This recipe section delves into the fascinating world of molecular gastronomy, inviting you to experiment with innovative techniques like spherification and foams. Get ready to surprise your senses and create dishes that are as visually stunning as they are delicious.

Ingredients:

The Alchemist's Toolkit (Choose your base):

- **For Spherification:**

  - 1 cup (240ml) fruit juice (such as mango, passion fruit, or pineapple)

  - 2.5 grams sodium alginate

  - Calcium lactate solution (dissolved in water according to package instructions)

- **For Foams:**

  - 1 cup (240ml) heavy cream (or vegan alternative)
  - 2 tablespoons powdered sugar (or substitute)
  - ½ teaspoon flavored extract (such as vanilla, almond, or coffee)
  - Lecithin (granules or liquid)

Additional Elements (Get Creative!):
- Fresh fruit for garnish
- Edible flowers (optional)
- Crumbled cookies or cake (optional)
- Chocolate sauce (optional)

Conversions:
- 1 cup = 240 ml (US customary) or 250 ml (metric)
- 1 tablespoon = 15 ml
- ½ teaspoon = 2.5 ml
- 2.5 grams = about ½ teaspoon

Special Equipment:

- **For Spherification:**

  - Measuring spoons and scale
  - Two large bowls
  - Spoon
  - Syringe or dropper

- **For Foams:**

  - Immersion blender or hand mixer
  - Whipped cream canister (optional)

Tips:
- Always handle sodium alginate and calcium lactate solutions with care.
- Use ripe fruit for the best flavor in spherification.
- Start with small batches when experimenting with foams to avoid over-whipping.

Allergy/Diet Differences:
- **Vegetarian:** Opt for vegetarian sources of calcium lactate, such as gluconodelta-lactone.
- **Vegan:** Use plant-based cream alternatives (such as coconut cream or soy cream) for foams. Choose vegan powdered sugar substitutes and lecithin derived from a vegan source.

Instructions:

The Alchemist's Choice (Spherification or Foams):

Spherification:

1. **Prepare the Sodium Alginate Bath:** In one large bowl, whisk together the fruit juice and sodium alginate until completely dissolved. Let it sit for 15 minutes to allow any air bubbles to rise and dissipate.
2. **Prepare the Calcium Lactate Bath:** Fill another large bowl with the calcium lactate solution according to package instructions.
3. **Form the Spheres:** Use a spoon or dropper to scoop small amounts of the fruit juice mixture and gently drop them into the calcium lactate bath. Let the spheres sit for 2-3 minutes, or until they harden completely.
4. **Drain and Rinse:** Carefully remove the spheres from the calcium lactate bath with a slotted spoon and rinse them briefly in clean water.

Foams:

1. **Combine the Ingredients:** In a chilled bowl, whisk together the heavy cream (or vegan alternative), powdered sugar, and flavored extract.
2. **Incorporate Air:** If using an immersion blender, insert it into the mixture and blend for about 30 seconds, or until frothy. Alternatively, use a hand mixer to whip the cream until soft peaks form.
3. **Stabilize the Foam (Optional):** For a more stable foam, add a pinch of lecithin granules or a few drops of liquid lecithin and gently fold it in.

Spirit's Touch (Plating and Presentation):

1. Arrange the prepared spheres or dollops of foam in a serving dish.
2. Get creative with your presentation! Add fresh fruit slices, edible flowers, crumbled cookies or cake, or a drizzle of chocolate sauce.

Serving Suggestions:
- Serve the molecular gastronomy creations immediately to enjoy the desired textures.
- Surprise your guests with these innovative and visually striking dishes!

Embrace the Spirit of Exploration!

This recipe section is just a springboard for your culinary adventures. Research different techniques like reverse spherification and explore various flavor combinations. Remember, the kitchen is your laboratory, and Spirit is your guide. Experiment, have fun, and create edible masterpieces that will amaze your senses!

Fusion Cuisine Creations (East Meets West and Beyond)

WELCOME TO THE REALM of Spirit, where we break down culinary borders and celebrate the magic of cultural fusion! This recipe section invites you to unleash your creativity and explore the exciting world of fusion cuisine. Let your inner alchemist take the wheel as you combine flavors and techniques from different regions to create innovative and delectable dishes.

Ingredients:

Fusion Inspiration (Choose your base and inspiration):

● **Base Protein (Choose one):**

○ 1 pound (450g) boneless, skinless chicken breasts or thighs

○ 1 pound (450g) salmon fillets

○ 1 pound (450g) ground beef or lamb

○ 1 block (14 ounces) firm tofu, drained and cubed (vegetarian option)

- **Fusion Inspiration (Choose your flavor profile):**

  ○ **Asian-European Fusion:**
  - 2 tablespoons soy sauce
  - 1 tablespoon rice vinegar
  - 1 tablespoon honey
  - 1 tablespoon Dijon mustard
  - 1 clove garlic, minced
  - 1 teaspoon grated ginger
  - ½ teaspoon sesame oil

  ○ **Latin-Asian Fusion:**
  - 2 tablespoons chipotle peppers in adobo sauce, chopped
  - 1 tablespoon fresh lime juice
  - 1 tablespoon orange juice
  - 1 teaspoon ground cumin
  - 1 teaspoon chili powder
  - ½ teaspoon smoked paprika

  ○ **Mediterranean-Asian Fusion:**
  - 2 tablespoons olive oil
  - 1 tablespoon lemon juice
  - 1 tablespoon chopped fresh oregano
  - 1 teaspoon dried thyme
  - 1 clove garlic, minced
  - ½ teaspoon red pepper flakes (optional)

Accompaniments (Get Creative!):
- Cooked rice or noodles
- Roasted vegetables
- Fresh herbs for garnish

Conversions:
- 1 pound = 450g
- 1 tablespoon = 15 ml
- ½ teaspoon = 2.5 ml

Tips:
- Marinate the chosen protein in your chosen fusion marinade for at least 30 minutes for deeper flavor.
- Experiment with different vegetables to complement your chosen flavor profile.
- Explore various cooking techniques like pan-frying, baking, or grilling to suit the protein and desired texture.

Allergy/Diet Differences:
- **Vegetarian:** Opt for the tofu base and choose a vegetarian-friendly fusion inspiration (such as Asian-inspired with a peanut sauce marinade).
- **Gluten-free:** Ensure all ingredients are certified gluten-free, especially the soy sauce (consider tamari) and marinades. Opt for gluten-free noodles or rice.

Instructions:

The Fusion Symphony:

1. In a shallow dish, combine the ingredients for your chosen fusion marinade. Add the chosen protein and marinate for at least 30 minutes, or up to overnight for deeper flavor.
2. Cook the marinated protein according to your preferred method (pan-frying, baking, or grilling).

Spirit's Touch (Plating and Presentation):

1. Serve the cooked protein over cooked rice or noodles.
2. Arrange roasted vegetables alongside the protein for a complete meal.
3. Garnish with fresh herbs for a touch of color and aroma.

Embrace the Spirit of Fusion!

This recipe section is a launchpad for your culinary exploration. Research different cuisines and their signature flavors. Get creative and don't be afraid to experiment with unexpected combinations. Remember, the world of fusion cuisine is vast and delicious, waiting to be discovered by your adventurous spirit!

Artistically Plated Desserts (A Symphony of Flavor and Form)

WELCOME TO THE REALM of Spirit, where creativity takes center stage! This recipe section delves into the world of artistically plated desserts, inviting you to transform simple ingredients into edible masterpieces. Let your imagination run wild as you explore unexpected flavor combinations and transform your plate into a canvas of color, texture, and taste.

Ingredients:

Foundation (Choose your base):

● **For Cakes and Tortes:**

○ Your favorite cake or torte recipe, baked and cooled according to package instructions or your preferred method.

● **For Mousses and Panna Cotta:**

○ Follow your preferred recipe for chocolate mousse, fruit mousse, or panna cotta, ensuring it sets properly.

- **For Fruit-Based Desserts:**

○ A selection of seasonal fruits (such as berries, stone fruits, citrus)
○ Fresh herbs (such as mint, basil) for garnish (optional)

Spirit's Palette (Flavor and Texture):
- **Sauces and Compotes:**

○ Fresh fruit compote (made with your favorite seasonal fruits)
○ Chocolate ganache (made with dark, milk, or white chocolate)
○ Caramel sauce (store-bought or homemade)

- **Sweet Accents:**

○ Whipped cream or coconut whipped cream
○ Edible flowers (optional)
○ Crushed nuts or cookies
○ Chocolate shavings
○ Powdered sugar

Conversions:
Refer to your chosen recipe for base desserts (cakes, mousses, etc.) for specific ingredient quantities and conversions.
Tips:
- Choose a base dessert that complements your chosen flavor profile and desired plating style.
- Use a variety of colors and textures to create visual interest on the plate.
- Utilize piping bags and stencils for creating decorative elements with sauces, whipped cream, or chocolate.
- Edible flowers add a touch of elegance and whimsy, but ensure they are safe for consumption.

Allergy/Diet Differences:
- **Vegan:** Opt for vegan cake, mousse, and panna cotta recipes. Use coconut whipped cream and choose vegan chocolate and sauces.
- **Gluten-free:** Ensure all ingredients, including the base dessert, are certified gluten-free. Consider using gluten-free cookie crumbles or toppings.
- **Dairy-free:** Use dairy-free alternatives for milk chocolate, whipped cream, and cheese (if using in a cheesecake base). Opt for coconut whipped cream and fruit-based sauces.

Instructions:
The Artist's Palette:

1. Prepare your chosen base dessert according to the recipe instructions. Allow it to cool completely before plating.
2. **For Cakes and Tortes:** Cut the cake or torte into desired shapes (squares, rounds, triangles) using cookie cutters or a sharp knife.
3. **For Mousses and Panna Cotta:** Unmold the set mousse or panna cotta and cut into portions, or scoop individual servings into bowls or small glasses.
4. **For Fruit-Based Desserts:** Wash and prepare your chosen fruits. Slice or arrange them artistically on a plate.

Spirit's Touch (Plating and Presentation):

1. Arrange the prepared dessert base on a serving plate.
2. Drizzle or spoon your chosen sauce (compote, ganache, caramel) around or over the dessert.
3. Pipe dollops of whipped cream or use a spoon to create decorative swirls.
4. Scatter your chosen sweet accents (nuts, cookies, chocolate shavings, powdered sugar) for pops of color and texture.
5. Garnish with fresh herbs or edible flowers (optional) to add a final touch of elegance.

Embrace the Spirit of Creativity!

This recipe section is a springboard for your artistic expression. Experiment with different flavor combinations, explore plating techniques, and let your imagination guide you. Remember, dessert is not just about taste; it's about creating a delightful experience for the eyes and the palate. So, unleash your inner artist and transform your desserts into edible works of art!

Edible Flower Salads (A Symphony of Color and Flavor)

WELCOME TO THE REALM of Spirit, where we celebrate the beauty and bounty of nature! This recipe section invites you to incorporate edible flowers into your salads, transforming them into edible works of art. Edible flowers add a touch of elegance, surprise, and unexpected flavors to your salad creations. Let your imagination bloom as you explore the vibrant world of edible flowers and craft salads that are as delightful to the eye as they are to the palate.

Ingredients:

● **Salad Foundation (Choose your favorites):**

○ 4 cups (mixed baby greens, chopped romaine, arugula, etc.)

○ 1 cup (assorted chopped vegetables such as cucumbers, tomatoes, bell peppers, fennel)

○ ½ cup (cooked and cooled protein - grilled chicken, shrimp, quinoa, chickpeas - optional)

○ ¼ cup (crumbled cheese - feta, goat cheese, blue cheese - optional)

● **Spirit's Bloom (Edible Flowers):**

○ ½ cup (assorted edible flowers such as pansies, violas, nasturtiums, calendula petals)

○ Fresh herbs (such as mint, basil, chives) for garnish (optional)

● **Vinaigrette Symphony (Dressing):**

○ ¼ cup (60ml) olive oil
○ 2 tablespoons (30ml) lemon juice or balsamic vinegar
○ 1 tablespoon (15ml) honey or maple syrup
○ Salt and freshly ground black pepper, to taste

Conversions:
● 1 cup = 240 ml (US customary) or 250 ml (metric)
● ¼ cup = 60 ml
● ½ cup = 120 ml
● 1 tablespoon = 15 ml

Tips:
● Select edible flowers from a reputable source that specializes in◇◇◇ (shokuyōka - edible flowers) or organic produce.
● Only use flowers that have been specifically identified as edible. Never consume flowers from your garden unless you are 100% certain they are safe.
● Harvest flowers early in the morning, just after the dew has dried.
● Edible flowers can be stored in the refrigerator for a day or two, but they are best enjoyed fresh.

Allergy/Diet Differences:
● **Vegetarian:** Omit the meat and opt for vegetarian protein sources like chickpeas, lentils, or tofu.
● **Vegan:** Exclude cheese and honey/maple syrup. Use a plant-based milk alternative (such as almond milk or coconut milk) for a creamier dressing. Opt for agave nectar or a touch of maple extract to add sweetness.

Instructions:

Building the Foundation:

1. Wash and prepare your chosen salad greens and vegetables. Arrange them in a large serving bowl.
2. If using cooked protein, add it to the salad bowl.
3. Crumble cheese over the salad (optional).

Spirit's Touch (Blooming the Salad):

1. Gently rinse the edible flowers, removing any debris.
2. Scatter the edible flowers over the prepared salad.
3. Garnish with fresh herbs (optional).

Vinaigrette Symphony (Dressing):

1. In a small bowl, whisk together the olive oil, lemon juice or balsamic vinegar, honey or maple syrup, salt, and

pepper to taste.

2. Drizzle the desired amount of dressing over the salad just before serving.

Serving Suggestions:

- Toss the salad gently to coat everything in the dressing before serving.
- Enjoy the beautiful and flavorful edible flower salad creation!

Embrace the Spirit of Exploration!

This recipe section is just a starting point for your edible flower adventures. Research different edible flowers and their flavor profiles. Explore flavor combinations and create signature salads that are bursting with color, taste, and a touch of magic. Remember, edible flowers are a delightful way to elevate your salads from ordinary to extraordinary!

Black Garlic Infused Dishes (A Symphony of Deep, Umami Flavors)

WELCOME TO THE REALM of Spirit, where we delve into the extraordinary! This recipe section explores the mysterious world of black garlic, an ingredient that transforms ordinary dishes into culinary masterpieces. Black garlic, with its inky cloves and complex flavor profile, adds a depth of umami unlike any other. Let your intuition guide you as you experiment with black garlic infusions, creating dishes that are both surprising and delectable.

Ingredients:

● **Black Garlic Magic (The Star Ingredient):**

○ Whole black garlic cloves, peeled (amount depending on the recipe)
○ Black garlic paste (substitute for fresh cloves, if desired)

Base Elements (Choose your canvas):

● **For Sauces and Spreads:**

○ Your favorite savory sauce recipe (such as marinara, pesto, mayonnaise)

● **For Soups and Stews:**

○ Broth of your choice (vegetable, chicken, beef)
○ Vegetables for your chosen soup or stew

● **For Mashed Potatoes and Risotto:**

○ Cooked potatoes or rice

● **For Main Courses (Optional):**

○ Protein of your choice (meat, seafood, tofu)

Spirit's Whisper (Additional Flavor Profiles):

● Fresh herbs (such as thyme, rosemary, parsley)
● Spices (such as smoked paprika, chili powder)
● Acid (such as lemon juice, balsamic vinegar)
● Cream or cheese (optional)

Conversions:

● 1 clove black garlic = about 5 grams

Tips:

● Black garlic has a strong, complex flavor. Start with a small amount and adjust to your taste.

● You can roast your own garlic cloves at a low temperature for several weeks to create black garlic, but buying it pre-made saves time.

● Black garlic is quite soft and spreadable. You can easily mash it into a paste for more convenient use.

Allergy/Diet Differences:

● **Vegetarian:** Omit meat or seafood and use vegetable broth for soups and stews. Opt for vegetarian protein options in main courses.

● **Vegan:** Use vegetable broth, vegan protein alternatives, and dairy-free substitutes like cashew cream or nutritional yeast for cream and cheese.

● **Gluten-free:** Ensure all ingredients are certified gluten-free, especially broths, sauces, and packaged products.

Instructions:
Black Garlic Magic (Infusing Different Dishes):
Sauces and Spreads:

1. Follow your preferred recipe for the chosen sauce or spread.
2. Before serving, stir in mashed black garlic cloves or black garlic paste to taste.

Soups and Stews:

1. Sauté chopped vegetables in a pot with olive oil.
2. Add your chosen broth and bring to a boil.
3. Reduce heat, simmer, and add a few whole black garlic cloves or a spoonful of black garlic paste.
4. Let the flavors meld for at least 30 minutes. Remove garlic cloves before serving (if using whole cloves).

Mashed Potatoes and Risotto:

1. Prepare mashed potatoes or risotto according to your preferred recipe.
2. Just before serving, stir in mashed black garlic cloves or black garlic paste for a depth of flavor.

Main Courses (Optional):

1. Marinate your chosen protein with olive oil, herbs, spices, a touch of acid, and mashed black garlic cloves or black garlic paste.
2. Cook the protein according to your preferred method (grilling, baking, pan-frying).
3. Brush the cooked protein with additional black garlic sauce or glaze (optional).

Spirit's Whisper (Customizing the Flavor Profile):
● Experiment with different herbs, spices, and acids to complement the black garlic's unique flavor.
● Dairy products like cream or cheese can add richness and complexity to black garlic infused dishes (consider vegan alternatives for dietary restrictions).

Serving Suggestions:
● Get creative! Black garlic can be infused into various dishes, adding a mysterious and umami twist to your culinary creations.
● Enjoy the surprising depth of flavor that black garlic brings to your favorite recipes.

Embrace the Spirit of Experimentation!
Black garlic opens a world of culinary exploration. Use it in unexpected ways, create unique flavor combinations, and infuse your dishes with the magic of Spirit. Remember, there are no rules – embrace your intuition and let black garlic guide you towards delicious discoveries!

A World of Molecular Cocktails (Boozy & Virgin Delights)

WELCOME TO THE REALM of Spirit, where we push boundaries and explore the transformative power of science in the beverage world! This recipe section delves into the fascinating world of molecular cocktails, inviting you to create visually stunning and innovative drinks. Experiment with techniques like spherification, foams, and smoking to elevate your cocktail game, but remember, the magic doesn't require alcohol! We'll also explore non-alcoholic options that are just as exciting and flavorful.

Ingredients:

The Alchemist's Toolkit (Choose your base):

● **For Alcoholic Cocktails:**

○ Spirits (such as vodka, gin, rum, tequila)

○ Liqueurs (optional)

○ Fresh fruits and herbs

○ Juices, syrups, and sodas

- **For Non-Alcoholic Cocktails:**

○ Sparkling water or soda
○ Fresh fruits and herbs
○ Juices, syrups, homemade fruit infusions (see tips)

Molecular Marvels (Choose your technique):
- **Spherification:**

○ Sodium alginate (dissolved in water according to package instructions)

○ Calcium lactate solution (dissolved in water according to package instructions)

○ Fruit juice or flavored syrup for the spheres

- **Foams:**

○ Heavy cream (or vegan alternative)
○ Flavored syrups or extracts
○ Lecithin (granules or liquid)

- **Smoking (Optional):**

○ Wood chips (such as applewood, cherrywood)
○ Smoking gun (or alternative smoking method)

Special Equipment:
- **Spherification:**

○ Measuring spoons and scale
○ Two large bowls
○ Spoon
○ Syringe or dropper

- **Foams:**

○ Immersion blender or hand mixer
○ Whipped cream canister (optional)

- **Smoking (Optional):**

○ Small metal tray
○ Tongs

Conversions:
- 1 cup = 240 ml (US customary) or 250 ml (metric)

- 1 tablespoon = 15 ml
- ½ teaspoon = 2.5 ml
- 2.5 grams = about ½ teaspoon

Tips:

- Always handle sodium alginate and calcium lactate solutions with care.
- Use ripe fruit for the best flavor in spherification.
- Start with small batches when experimenting with foams to avoid over-whipping.

Non-Alcoholic Delights:

- Create homemade fruit infusions by steeping fresh fruits in hot water for at least 30 minutes. Strain and use the resulting flavored water in your mocktails.
- Explore herbal infusions with fragrant herbs like rosemary, mint, or lavender.
- Spice up your virgin cocktails with a touch of ginger, chili flakes, or a squeeze of fresh citrus.

Allergy/Diet Differences:

- **Vegetarian:** Opt for vegetarian sources of calcium lactate, such as gluconodelta-lactone.
- **Vegan:** Use plant-based cream alternatives (such as coconut cream or soy cream) for foams. Choose vegan powdered sugar substitutes and lecithin derived from a vegan source. Opt for fruit-infused sparkling water or soda in non-alcoholic drinks.

Instructions:

The Alchemist's Choice (Alcoholic or Non-Alcoholic):

Alcoholic Cocktails:

Follow your favorite cocktail recipe, incorporating the chosen molecular technique (spherification, foams, smoking) for an extra touch of magic.

Non-Alcoholic Cocktails:

1. Combine your chosen base (sparkling water, soda, homemade fruit infusion) with fresh fruits, herbs, juices, and syrups to create your desired flavor profile.
2. Get creative with the molecular techniques! Make fruit spheres, add a delightful foam topping, or infuse your drink with smoke for a dramatic presentation.

Molecular Marvels (Putting on the Show):

Spherification:

1. Follow the instructions provided for spherification (see recipe section "Molecular Gastronomy Inspired Dishes").
2. Once the spheres are formed, gently add them to your finished cocktail for a burst of flavor and texture.

Foams:

1. Follow the instructions provided for foams (see recipe section "Molecular Gastronomy Inspired Dishes").
2. Gently spoon the flavored foam onto your finished cocktail for a beautiful and airy topping.

Smoking (Optional):

1. Soak wood chips in water for at least 30 minutes.
2. Light the wood chips in a small metal tray and use tongs to hold it over the glass. Alternatively, use a smoking gun following the manufacturer's instructions.

3.　Gently infuse the cocktail with smoke for a few seconds, then remove the tray or smoking gun.

Serving Suggestions:

● Serve your molecular cocktails in unique and elegant glassware, like coupe glasses, martini glasses, or footed glasses.

● Garnish with edible flowers, fresh fruit slices, or herbs for a touch of visual interest.

● Wow your guests with the playful presentation and surprising flavors of your creations!

Embrace the Spirit of Exploration!

This recipe section is just a springboard for your scientific and creative adventures in the beverage world. Research different molecular mixology techniques like reverse spherification and flavored dusts. Don't be afraid to experiment with flavor combinations and presentation styles. Remember, the bar is your laboratory, and Spirit is your guide! Craft show-stopping cocktails that are both delicious and visually stunning, be it with or without alcohol. Let your imagination run wild and create unforgettable drinking experiences for yourself and your guests!

Surprise Ingredient Dishes (Unconventional Twists and Flavor Delights)

WELCOME TO THE REALM of Spirit, where we break the mold and celebrate the magic of unexpected ingredients! This recipe section delves into the world of surprise ingredient dishes, inviting you to explore the exciting possibilities that lie beyond the ordinary. Let's embrace unconventional flavor combinations and transform familiar dishes with surprising twists.

Ingredients:

The Alchemist's Pantry (A World of Possibilities):

● **Classic Ingredients:**

  ○ Protein (chicken, fish, tofu, etc.)
  ○ Vegetables (a variety of your choice)
  ○ Grains (rice, quinoa, pasta, etc.)
  ○ Fruits (fresh or dried)

○ Dairy products (cheese, yogurt, etc.) (optional)

○ Pantry staples (olive oil, vinegar, soy sauce, etc.)

● **The Surprise Ingredient Stars:**

○ **Sweet and Savory:** Chocolate (dark, milk, white), coffee, fruits (such as mango, cherries), maple syrup, honey

○ **Umami and Earthy:** Miso paste, soy sauce, fish sauce, mushrooms, truffles (optional)

○ **Herbal and Spicy:** Fresh herbs (such as rosemary, thyme, cilantro), spices (such as curry powder, chipotle peppers), hot sauce

Conversions:

Refer to your chosen recipe for base ingredients (protein, vegetables, etc.) for specific ingredient quantities and conversions.

Tips:

● Start with a familiar dish and identify an element that could benefit from a surprising twist.

● Consider the flavor profile you want to achieve – sweet and savory, umami and earthy, or herbal and spicy.

● Introduce the surprise ingredient in small quantities at first, and adjust based on your taste preference.

Allergy/Diet Differences:

● **Vegetarian:** Opt for plant-based protein sources and exclude dairy products if necessary. Consider using a vegan cheese alternative.

● **Vegan:** Choose a plant-based protein and avoid dairy products and honey. Use maple syrup or agave nectar as a sweetener and opt for vegan chocolate if using chocolate as a surprise ingredient.

● **Gluten-free:** Ensure all ingredients are certified gluten-free, especially grains, sauces, and processed foods.

Instructions:

The Alchemist's Experiment (Building Your Surprise):

1. **Choose Your Base Dish:** Select a familiar recipe or dish that you enjoy.

2. **Identify the Surprise Opportunity:** Consider which element of the dish could benefit from an unexpected twist.

○ **Marinades:** Elevate your marinade with a touch of coffee, miso paste, or chopped fresh herbs.

○ **Sauces:** Introduce a surprising element like chocolate (for a mole sauce), fruit (for a chutney), or a touch of hot sauce for a spicy kick.

○ **Stuffings and Fillings:** Enhance your stuffing with dried fruits, chopped nuts, or even a sprinkle of cocoa powder for a rich flavor.

3. **Incorporate the Surprise Ingredient:**

○ Start with a small amount and gradually add more to achieve your desired flavor profile.

○ Be mindful of potential flavor clashes and ensure the surprise ingredient complements the overall dish.

Spirit's Inspiration: Unexpected Flavor Pairings

- **Dark Chocolate and Chili:** A match made in culinary heaven, adding a depth of complexity to savory dishes.
- **Miso and Roasted Vegetables:** The umami richness of miso beautifully complements the sweetness of roasted vegetables.
- **Coffee Rub on Steak:** Coffee grounds add a unique savory and slightly bitter depth to grilled steaks.
- **Blue Cheese and Fruit Salad:** The sharpness of blue cheese cuts through the sweetness of fruits, creating a delightful contrast.
- **Fresh Herbs and Fish:** Aromatic herbs like rosemary, thyme, and dill pair beautifully with all types of seafood.

Serving Suggestions:

- Plate your surprise ingredient dish creatively to add visual appeal.
- Garnish with fresh herbs, edible flowers (optional), or a drizzle of sauce for an extra touch of elegance.
- Surprise your guests with the unexpected and delightful flavor combinations!

Embrace the Spirit of Adventure!

The world of surprise ingredient dishes is an exciting playground for culinary exploration. Don't be afraid to experiment with unconventional pairings and embrace the magic of unexpected flavors. Remember, the kitchen is your laboratory, and Spirit is your guide! Unleash your creativity and craft dishes that are both surprising and delicious, leaving a lasting impression on your taste buds and those of your guests.

Interactive & Deconstructed Dishes (A Playful Exploration of Flavor and Form)

WELCOME TO THE REALM of Spirit, where we break free from convention and celebrate the joy of interactive dining! This recipe section delves into the world of interactive and deconstructed dishes, inviting you to create playful and engaging culinary experiences. Let's transform familiar flavors into a deconstructed playground, encouraging your guests to participate in the creation of their own unique bites.

Ingredients:

The Alchemist's Toolkit (Building Blocks):

- Focus on high-quality, fresh ingredients that can be easily assembled and customized by your guests.

- **Proteins:**

  ○ Seared steak, roasted chicken, grilled fish (sliced or cut into bite-sized pieces)

  ○ Tofu or tempeh (cubed and marinated) (vegetarian option)

- **Vegetables:**

  - Roasted vegetables (cut into bite-sized pieces)
  - Fresh vegetables (sliced or chopped) for dipping or assembling

- **Grains and Starches:**

  - Cooked rice, quinoa, couscous, or polenta
  - Bread or flatbreads for scooping and assembling

- **Sauces and Condiments:**

  - A variety of homemade or store-bought sauces, dips, and condiments to offer a range of flavors (consider vinaigrettes, chimichurri, pesto, yogurt sauce, hot sauce)

Spirit's Inspiration (Interactive Elements):
- **Bowls and Compartments:** Use divided plates, small bowls, or ramekins to create compartments for different elements of the dish.
- **Skewers and Picks:** Offer skewers or colorful picks for guests to assemble their own creations.
- **Interactive Toppings:** Provide various toppings like crumbled cheese, chopped nuts, fresh herbs, or edible flowers for customization.

Conversions:
Refer to your chosen recipe for base elements (proteins, vegetables, etc.) for specific ingredient quantities and conversions.

Tips:
- Consider the overall flavor profile when selecting ingredients. Ensure everything complements each other.
- Pre-cook all protein and vegetable elements to ensure a smooth and interactive dining experience.
- Arrange the deconstructed elements attractively on a platter or large serving board for visual appeal.

Allergy/Diet Differences:
- **Vegetarian:** Opt for plant-based proteins like tofu, tempeh, or lentils. Substitute dairy-based sauces with vegan alternatives like cashew cream or a yogurt-tahini sauce.
- **Vegan:** Choose vegan protein options and ensure all sauces and condiments are vegan-friendly.
- **Gluten-free:** Opt for gluten-free grains like quinoa, brown rice, or corn tortillas. Ensure all sauces, condiments, and pre-made items are certified gluten-free.

Instructions:
The Alchemist's Canvas (Creating the Deconstruction):

1. **Prepare the Base Elements:** Cook your chosen protein and vegetables according to your preferred method. Cut or shred them into bite-sized pieces for easy assembly.
2. **Cook Grains and Starches:** Prepare your chosen grain or starch according to package instructions.
3. **Assemble the Interactive Feast:** Arrange the prepped proteins, vegetables, grains/starches, sauces, and toppings on a large serving platter or individual plates with compartments.
4. **Get Creative!** Encourage your guests to use their imagination and assemble their own unique flavor combinations.

Serving Suggestions:

- Get creative with the presentation! Use decorative platters, colorful bowls, and fun serving utensils.
- Provide small plates or bowls for guests to create their own personalized portions.
- Encourage conversation and laughter as your guests interact with the food and each other.

Embrace the Spirit of Fun!

Interactive and deconstructed dishes are more than just a meal; they are an experience. Let go of formality and embrace the playful spirit of this culinary adventure. Remember, the kitchen is your playground, and Spirit is your guide! Craft a delightful and interactive dining experience that will leave your guests talking about it long after the last bite.

Part 6: The Power of Elemental Awareness - A Reflection on Your Culinary Journey

As you reach the culmination of your exploration through the elements in *Alchemy of the Oven*, it's time to reflect on the transformative power of elemental cooking. This journey wasn't just about mastering techniques or following recipes; it was about embracing a deeper understanding of the fundamental forces that shape our food and our culinary experiences.

Think back to your experiences with each element:

- **Earth:** How did working with root vegetables, grounding spices, and the nurturing warmth of the oven connect you to the foundation of a dish?

- **Air:** Did experimenting with lightness, aeration, and the delicate kiss of smoke elevate your appreciation for textural contrasts and ethereal flavors?

- **Fire:** Did the dance of flames, the searing sear, and the vibrant char on grilled foods ignite your passion for bold flavors and dynamic presentations?

- **Water:** Did the gentle simmer, the transformative power of broths, and the versatility of this essential element inspire you to create dishes that were both comforting and complex?

- **Spirit:** Did the exploration of unconventional pairings, surprise ingredients, and the freedom of experimentation awaken your inner culinary alchemist?

Elemental cooking has likely transformed your approach to food in several ways. Perhaps you now:

- **Appreciate the inherent balance and harmony** within a dish, where each element plays a crucial role.

- **Approach recipe creation with a newfound sense of intuition**, using the elements as a guiding force.

- **View familiar ingredients with fresh eyes**, recognizing their elemental properties and the potential they hold.

- **Embrace a more playful and experimental spirit in the kitchen**, confident in your ability to control and combine the elements.

As you continue your culinary journey, remember the power of elemental awareness. Let it guide you in your exploration of new cuisines, techniques, and ingredients. Never stop questioning, experimenting, and most importantly, having fun!

The fire of your passion, the air of your creativity, the water of your adaptability, the earth of your grounding knowledge, and the spirit of your unique perspective – these are the elements that will continue to shape your culinary alchemy.

Keep exploring, keep creating, and keep embracing the magic in the kitchen!

Unleashing Your Inner Alchemist: Tips for Creating Your Own Elemental Dishes

AS YOU EMBARK ON YOUR own culinary adventures beyond the pages of *Alchemy of the Oven*, remember that the true magic lies in experimentation and the expression of your unique culinary spirit. Here are some tips to guide you in creating your own elemental dishes:

Embrace the Elemental Framework:

- **Don't be confined by strict interpretations:** Use the elements as a guiding force, not a rigid set of rules.
- **Focus on the essence of each element:** Consider how the qualities of **Earth** (grounding), **Air** (lightness), **Fire** (transformation), **Water** (fluidity), and Spirit (unconventionality) can be expressed in your dishes.

Experiment with Techniques:

- **Explore different cooking methods:** Roasting (**Earth**), whipping (**Air**), searing (**Fire**), poaching (**Water**), and molecular techniques (**Spirit**) can all be used to manipulate the elements within your dish.
- **Don't be afraid to combine elements:** Create dishes that showcase the interplay between fire-roasted vegetables and a light, airy espuma (foam) sauce (**Air & Fire**).

Be Playful with Ingredients:

- **Seek out seasonal and local ingredients:** Let the inherent qualities of the ingredients guide your elemental choices.
- **Embrace surprise ingredients:** Introduce a touch of Spirit by incorporating an unexpected element, like chocolate in a savory dish (Earth & Spirit).

Presentation Matters:

- **Plate your dishes with intention:** Use color, texture, and arrangement to visually represent the elements at play.
- **Engage your guests' senses:** Create an interactive dining experience that invites them to explore the elemental interplay on their plates.

Embrace the Journey:

- **Don't be afraid to make mistakes:** See them as opportunities to learn and refine your elemental understanding.
- **Most importantly, have fun!** Cooking should be a joyful and creative experience.

Remember, the kitchen is your laboratory, and you are the alchemist! Use the elemental framework as a springboard for your culinary creativity. Craft dishes that are not only delicious but also a reflection of your unique spirit and vision.

Keep experimenting, keep exploring, and keep pushing the boundaries of your culinary alchemy!

Alchemy of the Oven: Elemental Pantry Guide

STOCK YOUR KITCHEN with these elemental essentials to empower your culinary alchemy and craft dishes that resonate with the forces of nature!

Earth:

- **Root Vegetables:** Potatoes, carrots, beets, sweet potatoes, onions, garlic (grounding, sweetness, savory depth)
- **Whole Grains:** Brown rice, quinoa, farro (nuttiness, texture, nourishment)
- **Legumes:** Lentils, beans (protein, heartiness, earthiness)
- **Nuts and Seeds:** Almonds, walnuts, pumpkin seeds (healthy fats, richness, texture)
- **Warm Spices:** Ground cumin, coriander, turmeric, cinnamon (warmth, depth of flavor)
- **Dried Herbs:** Thyme, rosemary, sage (earthy notes, fragrance)

Air:

- **Eggs:** (essential for aeration, structure, emulsification)
- **Cream:** Heavy cream for whipping, lighter creams for sauces (richness, lightness, texture)
- **Leavening Agents:** Baking powder, baking soda, yeast (lift, air incorporation)
- **Fruits (fresh and dried):** Berries, apples, citrus fruits (freshness, sweetness, acidity)
- **Light Herbs:** Fresh parsley, dill, chives (delicate flavors, pops of color)

Fire:

- **High-Smoke Point Oils:** Canola oil, avocado oil (suitable for high-heat cooking)

- **Vinegars:** Red wine vinegar, balsamic vinegar (acidity, brightness, depth of flavor)
- **Chiles (fresh and dried):** Fresh chilies for heat, dried chilies for smokiness and depth (heat, spice, complexity)
- **Hot Peppers:** Cayenne pepper, red pepper flakes (adjustable heat)
- **Strong Spices:** Cayenne pepper, black pepper, chipotle peppers (heat, smoky notes)

Water:

- **Broths:** Chicken broth, vegetable broth (flavor base, moisture)
- **Stocks:** Beef stock, seafood stock (richer, more complex flavor base)
- **Acids:** Lemon juice, lime juice (acidity, brightness, balance)
- **Sugars:** Granulated sugar, brown sugar (sweetness, caramelization)
- **Fats (for Sauces):** Butter, olive oil (fat base, richness, smoothness)

Spirit:

- **Surprise Ingredients:** Chocolate (bittersweet, milk, white), coffee, miso paste, fish sauce (unexpected flavors, complexity)
- **Fresh Herbs (variety):** Experiment beyond the basics (unique flavor profiles, pops of color)
- **Specialty Vinegars:** Champagne vinegar, sherry vinegar (unique acidity, complexity)
- **Floral Waters:** Rosewater, orange flower water (subtle floral notes, intrigue)
- **Seasoning Salts:** Furikake, za'atar (unique flavor profiles, global inspiration)

Alchemy of the Oven: Glossary of Terms

THIS GLOSSARY DEFINES key culinary terms used throughout the book to enhance your understanding and empower your exploration of elemental cooking.

Air

- **Aeration:** Incorporating air into a substance to create a lighter texture, often achieved through whipping or folding techniques.
- **Emulsion:** A stable mixture of two immiscible liquids (like oil and water) achieved through an emulsifying agent (like egg yolk or lecithin).
- **Espuma (Foam):** A light and airy foam created by whipping a flavored liquid with a stabilizing agent.

Earth

- **Braise:** A slow cooking method that involves browning food in a small amount of fat and then simmering it in a covered pot with liquid.
- **Mirepoix:** A flavor base made by finely chopping equal parts onion, carrot, and celery.
- **Roux:** A thickening agent made by cooking equal parts fat (butter) and flour until a paste forms.

Fire

- **Caramelize:** Heating sugar until it melts and turns a golden brown color, adding sweetness and depth of flavor.
- **Maillard Reaction:** The chemical reaction between amino acids and reducing sugars that occurs at high temperatures, creating browned flavors and aromas (searing).
- **Sear:** Cooking food quickly over high heat to create a browned crust and seal in juices.

Water

- **Blanch:** Briefly cooking food in boiling water to soften it or stop the cooking process.
- **Hydrocolloids:** Thickening and gelling agents derived from plants, seaweed, or microbial cultures (agar agar, xanthan gum).
- **Poach:** Cooking food gently in simmering liquid to preserve its delicate texture.

General

- **Conversion:** Adjusting ingredient quantities based on unit measurements (grams to cups, etc.).
- **Infuse:** Steeping an ingredient in a liquid to impart its flavor (example: herbs in oil).
- **Suprema:** The boneless, skinless supreme of a chicken or fish is the tenderloin muscle.

Spirit

- **Deconstructed Dish:** A dish where the individual components are presented separately, allowing diners to assemble their own bites.
- **Molecular Gastronomy:** The scientific exploration of the physical and chemical processes that occur during cooking.
- **Spherification:** A technique for creating small spheres filled with a liquid or puree using sodium alginate and calcium lactate.

Don't miss out!

Visit the website below and you can sign up to receive emails whenever Emilee Avink publishes a new book. There's no charge and no obligation.

https://books2read.com/r/B-A-OHAFB-LKSID

BOOKS2READ

Connecting independent readers to independent writers.

Did you love *Alchemy of the Oven: Earth, Air, Fire, Water, Spirit*? Then you should read *Embracing the Witch's Shadow: A Guide to Transformation and Self-Discovery: Unlocking the Secrets of Witchcraft, Healing and Personal Empowerment*[1] by Emilee Avink!

"Exploring the Witch's Shadow: A Simple Guide for Change and Finding Yourself" offers an exciting trip. This book easily mixes old teachings with modern ways of finding yourself, acting as a key to your deepest self. At its heart, it reveals the skill of shadow work with a witch's touch, leading you down a path of healing, growing, and becoming stronger.Whether you're a seasoned pro or just starting, everyone can use this all-in-one method. The book offers 400 thought-provoking questions across 20 topics, making it a handy map for looking inward, healing, and finding yourself. Plus, you'll learn about crystals, herbs, special ceremonies, how to meditate, tarot card reading, and more to grow your magical skills.The book centers around ethical witchcraft, matching your journey with values and wellness. Get ready for a magical trip of finding and growing yourself, experiencing both light and dark sides. Discover your hidden strength and endless possibilities on this magical trip.

---

1. https://books2read.com/u/bQpL6d

2. https://books2read.com/u/bQpL6d

Also by Emilee Avink

Embracing the Witch's Shadow: A Guide to Transformation and Self-Discovery: Unlocking the Secrets of Witchcraft,
Healing and Personal Empowerment
Where Two Worlds Collide
The Infinite Loop: A Time Traveler's Search for Love
Whispers of the Guardian: Haleema's Legacy
The Pot of Plenty: Stretching Your Dollar with 50 Delicious Rice and Bean Dishes
Description for Nine Lives of Magic: Working with Your Feline Familiar
Once Upon a Feast: Fairytale Treats for Little Chefs
The Glitching Grimoire: A Tech Witch's Guide to Digital Spellcraft
The Healing Table: Crystal-Infused Meals
Buzzing with Magic: Quick & Effective Witchcraft for Busy Bees
The Witch's Daily Cup: Rituals and Recipes for Coffee Magic
Alchemy of the Oven: Earth, Air, Fire, Water, Spirit